PRACTICAL
BUSINESS

차형석

- 한국외국어대학교 졸업
- 미국 필라델피아 Drexel LeBow MBA 졸업
- 한양대학교 국제학대학원 박사과정
- 삼성전자 국제 프로젝트 협상 전문가 (월트 디즈니, 소니, 파나소닉과 대형 프로젝트 협상)
- LG전자 대외 협력 사업 담당 (다국적 기업과의 비즈니스 협상 및 국제회의 통역)
- 번역서: 〈올림픽 인사이드〉, 〈이노베이터 진실게임〉, 〈고객 충성의 신화〉
- 저서: 〈비즈니스 영어 핵심 패턴 233〉 등

English for Business Communication

Practical Business 사내 실무 영어

지은이 차형석
펴낸이 정규도
펴낸곳 (주)다락원

초판 1쇄 발행 2008년 11월 10일
2판 1쇄 발행 2019년 11월 29일
2판 4쇄 발행 2024년 1월 10일

편집총괄 장의연
책임편집 유나래
표지 디자인 하태호
본문 디자인 HADA 장선숙
전산 편집 이현해
삽화 김인화
사진 shutterstock

다락원 경기도 파주시 문발로 211
내용문의: (02)736-2031 내선 523
구입문의: (02)736-2031 내선 250~252
Fax: (02)732-2037
출판등록 1977년 9월 16일 제406-2008-000007호

ISBN 978-89-277-0118-7 13740

http://www.darakwon.co.kr

- 다락원 홈페이지를 방문하시면 상세한 출판정보와 함께 여러 도서의 동영상강좌, MP3자료 등 다양한 어학 정보를 얻으실 수 있습니다.

PRACTICAL
BUSINESS

사내 실무 영어

Heungsok Cha

DARAKWON

영어는 마라톤이다.
쉬지 말고 꾸준히 달려라!

언젠가 수영을 정식으로 배운 적이 있다. 운동 신경이 조금 있던 나는 자유형과 배영은 그다지 큰 어려움 없이 소화해낼 수 있었다. 그러나 정작 내가 가장 잘하고 싶었던 종목은 평영이었다. 평영이 겉보기에는 개구리가 꼼지락거리는 것처럼 보인다고 하지만 내게는 은근히 매력 있어 보이는 영법이었다. 그러나 발길질만 배우는 데 한 달을 소비했는데도 앞으로 나가지를 못해 답답해진 나는 나름대로의 노하우(?)를 만들어가기 시작했다. 그랬더니 어느 날 갑자기 앞으로 나가기 시작하는 것이 아닌가! 그러나 문제는 그 이후로는 아무리 열심히 해도 속도가 더 이상 붙지 않았다는 점이다. 정식으로 배운 학생들은 날 앞지르기 시작했고 나는 더 이상 그들의 상대가 되지 못했다. 바로 제대로 배우지 않았기 때문이었다. 이때 한 번 더 깨달았다. 모든 일에는 정도(正道)가 있다는 것을……

영어란 녀석도 마찬가지인 듯 싶다. 좀 더 빨리 잘해보고자 나름의 요령을 피우지만, 결국 그것이 지름길이 아님을 뼈저리게 느끼게 된다. 영어는 우리에게 쉽게 백기를 들지 않는 자존심 강한 놈이다. 강함은 꾸준함과 부드러움으로 상대해야 한다.

필자는 이 책을 통해 여러분께 비즈니스 영어의 정도를 제공하고자 한다. 현장에서 경험한 나의 비즈니스 영어는 이 책을 집필하는 데 커다란 자산이 되었다. 즉, 이 책에서 여러분이 만나게 될 표현은 반드시 실전에서 필요한 표현이라는 것이다. 조급한 마음에 모든 표현을 외우고 암기하겠다는 생각보다는 표현을 이해하고 실제로 벌어질 수 있는 상황을 머릿속에 그려가면서 익혀보자. 그러면 훨씬 오래도록 기억에 남게 될 것이다.

꾸준한 노력과 연습만이 영어를 내 것으로 만들고 능숙해지는 올바른 길일 것이다. 그 정도(正道)는 몇 년이 걸리는 머나먼 여행일 수 있다. 그러나 정도에서 벗어나지 않고 계속 걷다 보면 영어라는 독종도 우리에게 쉬어갈 수 있는 조그만 쉼터를 제공하기 시작할 것이다.

이제 당신은 앞으로 42.195km 거리를 힘차게 뛰어야 하는 출발선에 서 있다. 다시 한 번 호흡을 가다듬고 꾸준한 페이스로 전진해 나가서 완주하라. 이 책이 바로 그 출발선이다. 영어는 마라톤이다.

차형석

Contents

Overview

PART 1 비즈니스 회의 Business Meetings

Week	Title	Overview
WEEK 01	회의 소집 및 안건 소개 Calling a Meeting and Addressing the Agenda	• 회의 관련 기본 어휘 익히기 Learning basic vocabulary for meetings • 회의 소집하기 Calling a meeting • 안건 소개하기 Introducing agenda items
WEEK 02	안건 토의하기 Discussing the Agenda	• 효과적으로 회의 시작하기 Starting a meeting effectively • 의견 말하기 Expressing opinions • 안건에 대한 의견 묻기 Asking for opinions about the agenda
WEEK 03	회의 통제하기 및 끝맺기 Controlling and Wrapping up a Meeting	• 끼어드는 법 익히기 Learning how to interrupt • 회의 통제하기 Controlling a meeting • 요약하고 회의 끝맺기 Summarizing and wrapping up a meeting
PLUS WEEK	동의하기 및 반대하기 Agreeing and Disagreeing	• 동의 표시하기 Expressing agreement • 반대 표시하기 Expressing disagreement • 의견 강조하기 Emphasizing opinions

PART 2 비즈니스 프레젠테이션 Business Presentations

Week	Title	Overview
WEEK 04	발표 목적과 발표자 소개 Introducing the Goal of the Presentation and the Presenter	• 발표자 소개하기 Introducing a presenter • 발표 목적 알리기 Informing about the purpose of the presentation • 발표 절차 안내하기 Explaining the procedure of the presentation
WEEK 05	발표 시작과 전개 Starting and Developing a Presentation	• 효과적으로 발표 시작하기 Starting a presentation effectively • 발표 전개하기 Developing a presentation • 주제 전환하기 Switching topics
WEEK 06	발표 마무리하기 및 질문받기 Concluding a Presentation and Taking Questions	• 주요 사항 요약하기 Summarizing main points • 발표 마무리하기 Concluding a presentation • 질문에 답하기 Answering questions
PLUS WEEK	시각자료 사용 및 효과적인 분석 Visual Aids and Effective Analysis	• 시각자료 소개하기 Showing visual aids • 효과적으로 자료 분석하기 Analyzing the visuals effectively • 논리적으로 발표하기 Making logical presentations

SPECIAL PART 비즈니스 이메일 Business E-mail

Unit	Title	Overview
UNIT 01	의견 묻고 나누기 Asking and Sharing Opinions	• 의견 요청하기 Asking for opinions • 의견 말하기 Giving opinions • 의견 진술 회피하기 Avoiding giving opinions
UNIT 02	동의하기 또는 반대하기 Agreeing or Disagreeing	• 동의하기 Agreeing • 반대하기 Disagreeing • 대안 제시하기 Proposing alternatives

Practical Business
Business Meetings

PART 1
비즈니스 회의

회의 소집 및 안건 소개

Calling a Meeting and Addressing the Agenda

Vocabulary & Expressions

회의 관련 어휘

- **meeting** 회의
- **urgent meeting** 긴급 회의
- **agenda** 의제, 협의사항 / **agenda items** 안건
- **minutes** 회의록
- **topic** (회의의) 주제, 화제 (= subject)
- **refreshments** 다과, 가벼운 음식

- **discussion** 논의 (discuss 논의하다)
- **last for + 시간** ~동안 지속하다, 계속하다 (= take + 시간)
- **cover** (주제를) 다루다, 포함하다 (= deal with)
- **attend** 참석하다
- **set up a meeting** 회의를 잡다 (set up = call, arrange)
- **take a break** 휴식을 갖다

회의 목적 말하기

- **The purpose of the meeting is to** 회의의 목적은 ~하는 것입니다 (purpose = objective)
- **We are meeting today to / We are here today to** 우리는 ~하기 위해 오늘 모였습니다
- **What we want to do here is to** 여기서 우리가 하고자 하는 것은 ~입니다
- **The meeting is supposed to focus on** 회의는 ~에 중점을 두고 있습니다
- **The meeting is about** 회의는 ~에 관한 것입니다

회의 안건 말하기

- **Today's agenda is** 오늘 회의의 의제는 ~입니다
- **... is on the table[agenda]** ~이 의제에 올라와 있습니다
- **I'd like to talk about** ~에 대해 이야기 나누고 싶습니다

> **Plus Tip**
>
> 회의 소집하기 전 체크리스트
>
> - **Define the objective** 목적 정하기
> - **Set up a date and place** 날짜와 장소 정하기
> - **Check who's attending** 참석자 확인하기
> - **Prepare the equipment and papers** 장비 및 서류 준비하기

Useful Expressions

I suppose I could call a meeting.	회의를 소집해야겠습니다.
We need to discuss how to work more effectively.	좀 더 효과적으로 일하는 방법에 대해서 **논의해볼 필요가 있어요**.
Can you make it on Wednesday?	수요일에 **참석할 수 있어요?**
Can I add one more item to the agenda?	의제에 하나 더 **추가해도 될까요?**
How long will the meeting last?	회의는 **얼마나 걸리죠?**

A Match the meanings on the left with the expressions on the right.

1 짧은 휴식 ·   · ⓐ the objective of the meeting

2 회의 목적 ·   · ⓑ urgent meeting

3 안건 ·   · ⓒ short break

4 논의 ·   · ⓓ discussion

5 긴급 회의 ·   · ⓔ agenda items

B Fill in the blanks using the given words.

1 5월 7일에 회의를 잡았으면 합니다.
   ▶ I want to _____ a meeting on May 7.

2 월례 회의의 목적은 우리의 TV 광고에 대해 논의하는 것입니다.
   ▶ The _____ of the monthly meeting is to _____ our TV commercial.

3 마케팅 문제가 의제에 올라와 있습니다.
   ▶ The marketing issue is on the _____.

4 회의는 약 50분 동안 계속될 것입니다.
   ▶ The meeting will _____ for about 50 minutes.

5 목요일에 회의에 참석할 수 있어요?
   ▶ Can you _____ the meeting _____ Thursday?

> Words
> last
> attend
> discuss
> purpose
> on
> arrange
> table

C Refer to the Korean and fill in the blanks.

1 We will have a _____ _____ after discussing the first agenda item.
   첫 번째 안건을 논의한 후에 커피를 들며 휴식을 갖겠습니다.

2 _____ we _____ to do today is to finalize our budget.
   오늘 우리가 하고자 하는 것은 예산을 확정하는 일입니다.

3 All the members must _____ the _____ meeting.
   전원이 긴급 회의에 참석해야 합니다.

4 We have three _____ to _____ regarding our ordering process.
   우리의 주문 절차와 관련해 논의할 사항이 세 가지 있습니다.

5 We haven't been informed of the _____ _____.
   회의 의제에 대해 알고 있는 바가 없습니다.

01.mp3

A Well, I suppose I could call a meeting.

B ¹**What's the purpose of** the meeting, Thomas?

A ²**We need to talk about** next month's production schedule. Can you make it on Wednesday?

B Sorry, ³**it looks like** Wednesday will be difficult. I'm scheduled to meet with a client. How about Thursday morning?

A Thursday morning sounds okay. Then let's get together in room 401 at 10.

B Okay. I'll let my team members know. I'll see you then.

Pattern Training

1 **What's the purpose of** [＿＿＿＿＿＿]**?** ~의 목적이 무엇이죠?

① the quarterly meeting
② the press conference
③ the urgent meeting

▶ 분기 회의 / 기자 회견 / 긴급 회의

2 **We need to talk about** [＿＿＿＿＿＿]**.** ~에 관해 이야기할 필요가 있어요.

① our sick leave policy
② how to improve our working environment
③ why this project is being delayed

▶ 우리의 병가 규정 / 우리의 작업 환경을 개선하는 방법 / 이 프로젝트가 왜 늦어지고 있는지

3 **It looks like** [＿＿＿＿＿＿]**.** ~한 것처럼 보입니다.

① we need a meeting
② the meeting place has changed
③ our boss was not satisfied with the results

▶ 회의가 필요한 것 / 회의 장소가 변경된 것 / 상사가 그 결과에 만족하지 않은 것

02.mp3

A [1]**Thank you all so much for** coming. We have two items to cover on the agenda today. One is selecting the employee of the months, and the other is hiring more engineers.

B Can I add one more item to the agenda?

A Sure. Go ahead.

B I'd like to talk about adding more assembly lines.

A I don't see why not. [2]**We will discuss that** later in the meeting.

C How long will the meeting last?

A It will last for about two hours. And [3]**we will take a** 10-minute **break** before we proceed to the second agenda item.

Pattern Training

1 **Thank you all so much for** [_____]. ~에 대해 모두에게 정말 감사 드립니다.

① participating
② attending
③ coming all the way down here

▶ 참석해주신 것 / 참석해주신 것 / 여기까지 먼 길을 와주신 것

2 **We will discuss that** [_____]. 그것을 ~ 다룰 겁니다.

① again next week
② briefly here
③ with more details in Dallas in December

▶ 다음 주에 다시 / 여기서 간략하게 / 댈러스에서 12월에 좀 더 자세히

3 **We will take a** [_____] **break.** ~ 휴식을 가질 겁니다.

① coffee
② lunch
③ 5-minute

▶ 커피를 마시면서 / 점심식사 동안 / 5분간

○ More Expressions

회의 소요 시간 묻기

· How long will the meeting **last**?
· How long will the meeting **take**?
· How long will the meeting **run**?
회의는 얼마나 **걸리죠**?

A Fill in the blanks using the given words.

add	agenda	look
minutes	difficult	cover

1 A: Mr. Baker, could you take the _____?

  B: Sure, I can.

  베이커 씨, 회의록을 기록해주시겠어요? – 그러죠, 하겠습니다.

2 A: As you can see from the _____, there're three items.

  B: Oh, can I _____ one more?

  의제에서 보시다시피, 세 개의 토의 안건이 있습니다. – 아, 하나 더 추가해도 될까요?

3 A: Can you make the meeting on Monday?

  B: Sorry, but it _____ like Monday is going to be _____.

  월요일에 회의에 참석하실 수 있으세요? – 죄송하지만, 월요일은 어려울 것 같아요.

4 A: Today, we have three items to _____.

  B: What are they?

  오늘은 다룰 사항이 세 가지 있습니다. – 그게 뭐죠?

B Put the Korean into English and complete the short dialogs.

1

A: 회의를 열었으면 합니다. (want / arrange)

B: Why is that?

A: We need to make a quick decision on some new sales techniques.
언제 모이는 게 좋을까요? (good time / get together)

B: How about 4 o'clock?

A: Okay. Then I'll arrange a meeting at 4 and hand out the necessary documents beforehand.

2

A: Thank you for coming here.

B: 회의의 목적이 뭐죠? (what / purpose)

A: As you know, we aren't meeting our deadlines for most orders recently.

B: That's right. Many customers are complaining about that.

A: 그래서 주문을 더 빨리 처리하는 방법을 논의해보고자 우리가 여기에 모인 겁니다.
(we are here to / process / quickly)

A Listen to the dialog and answer the questions.   03.mp3

1 What's the purpose of the meeting? ▶ _____

2 How long will the meeting last? ▶ _____

3 How many agenda items do they have to discuss? ▶ _____

4 When are they planning to take a break? ▶ _____

B Listen again and complete the blanks.   03.mp3

Sophia: Thank you for coming ¹_____ _____ _____ . I've asked you here because ²_____ _____ _____ _____ several changes to our company policy.

Donald: What time do you think ³_____ _____ _____ _____?

Sophia: ⁴_____ _____ _____ how well we understand each other's position.

Donald: Okay.

Sophia: ⁵_____ _____ _____ _____ is the sick leave policy, and the second one is the overtime work policy. We will ⁶_____ _____ _____ _____ after discussing the first one.

C Listen to the dialog and check true or false.   04.mp3

	True	False
1 The man did not check his email.		
2 The meeting is about product designs.		
3 The meeting is this afternoon.		
4 The meeting will be held in Meeting Room 3.		

+ BIZ TIPs 회의 종류

▶ **주제에 따른 분류**

board meeting 임원 회의
shareholders' meeting 주주 회의
business meeting 사업 회의
production meeting 생산 회의
marketing meeting 마케팅 회의
product planning meeting 상품 기획 회의

▶ **빈도에 따른 분류**

regular meeting 정기 회의
irregular meeting 부정기 회의
weekly meeting 주간 회의
monthly meeting 월례 회의
quarterly meeting 분기 회의
yearly meeting 연간 회의

안건 토의하기

Discussing the Agenda

Vocabulary & Expressions

논의 시작하기

- **Let's get down to business.** 본론으로 들어갑시다.
- **The issue is about** 쟁점은 ~에 관한 것입니다
- **Why don't we begin with ...?** ~부터 시작하는 것이 어떨까요?
- **Let's start with** ~부터 시작합시다
- **Let's start by outlining** ~을 개요부터 설명하는 것으로 시작합시다

재확인하기

- **What do you mean by ...?** ~이 무슨 뜻이죠?
- **So, what you're saying is ...?** 그러니까 당신의 말은 ~라는 거죠?
- **So, your point is that ...?** 그러니까 당신의 요지는 ~입니까?
- **If I'm not wrong, your concern is ...?**
  제가 틀리지 않았다면, 당신이 염려하는 부분이 ~인가요?

의견 말하기

- **I think / I believe** ~라고 생각합니다
- **It seems to me that** ~인 것 같습니다
- **In my opinion, / In my view, / As I see it, / As far as I'm concerned,** 제 생각에는,
- **Maybe we could** ~해볼 수도 있을 겁니다
- **Why don't we ...? / How about ...?** ~하는 게 어때요?
- **My point is that** 제 요지는 ~입니다
- **I believe we should** 우리가 ~해야 한다고 생각해요
- **We need to** 우리는 ~해야 할 필요가 있습니다
- **It is obvious that** ~라는 점은 명백합니다
- **I feel very strongly that** ~라고 굳게 믿습니다
- **I suggest that / I recommend that** ~을 제안합니다

의견 묻기

- **What do you think of[about] ...? / How do you feel about ...?**
  ~에 대해 어떻게 생각하세요?
- **What is your opinion of[about] ...?**
  ~에 대한 당신 의견은 어때요? (opinion = view)
- **Do you have any suggestions?**
  제안사항 있으세요?
- **Could we hear from *someone* on ...?**
  …에 대해서 ~의 의견을 들어볼 수 있을까요?

Useful Expressions

- Let's start with the issue that Becky raised.
  베키가 제기한 사안**부터 시작합시다.**

- According to the survey, our market share has dropped.
  그 조사**에 의하면**, 우리의 시장점유율이 떨어졌습니다.

- Could we hear from Susan about that?
  그 점에 대해 수잔**의 의견을 들어볼 수** 있을까요?

- I believe we should amend our regulations.
  우리의 규정을 수정해야 한다고 **생각합니다.**

- In my opinion, we need to discuss it with top management.
  제 생각에는, 최고 경영진과 그것을 논의할 필요가 있습니다.

Vocabulary Check-Up

A Match the meanings on the left with the expressions on the right.

1 실수 없이 ·   · ⓐ cost reduction

2 초과 근무 시간 ·   · ⓑ without an error

3 비용 삭감 ·   · ⓒ on a monthly basis

4 월 단위로 ·   · ⓓ overtime hours

5 연구, 조사 ·   · ⓔ research

B Fill in the blanks with the given words.

1 제가 틀리지 않다면, 당신이 염려하는 바는 숙련된 인력이 부족하다는 거죠?
  ▶ If I'm not _____, your _____ is our lack of skilled manpower?

2 우리의 마케팅 전략을 수정하는 게 어때요?
  ▶ _____ don't we amend our marketing strategy?

3 우리의 매출 목표가 달성될 수 없다는 것은 명백합니다.
  ▶ It is _____ that our sales goals cannot be reached.

4 제 생각에는, 우리의 근무 환경을 좀 더 잘 관리해야 합니다.
  ▶ In _____ _____, we should take better care of our working environment.

5 그러니까 당신이 말하고자 하는 게 컴퓨터 네트워크를 업그레이드해야 한다는 건가요?
  ▶ So, _____ you're _____ is we need to upgrade our computer network?

> Words
> what
> saying
> opinion
> wrong
> my
> obvious
> concern
> why

C Refer to the Korean and fill in the blanks.

1 What is _____ _____ about this?
  이 점에 대한 당신 의견은 어때요?

2 It _____ to me that the primary goals of the company _____ to be clarified.
  회사의 주요 목표가 분명해질 필요가 있는 것 같아요.

3 As far _____ I'm _____, we should lower the price.
  제 생각에는, 가격을 낮춰야 합니다.

4 I _____ it is important to be able to _____ over 2,000 units on a monthly basis.
  매월 2천 개 이상을 생산할 수 있는 능력이 중요하다고 생각합니다.

5 Do you have _____ _____ that might help in solving this problem?
  이 문제를 해결하는 데 도움이 될 만한 제안사항 있으세요?

05.mp3

A ¹**Let's start with** the first item. It is about cost reduction. Sammy, I know that you've prepared a report on this issue.

B Yes, I have.

A Why don't you start?

B Okay. According to my research, we've been spending too much money on indirect costs such as security.

A So, do you have any suggestions that would help us reduce them?

B Sure. ²**I believe we should** change our current security system. The current one costs us a lot of money to maintain.

A I see. ³**Could we hear from** Susan about that?

Pattern Training

1　**Let's start with** ☐. ~부터 시작합시다.

① the easy stuff first
② a simple bar graph
③ some background information
▶ 우선 쉬운 것 / 단순한 막대 그래프 / 약간의 배경 정보

2　**I believe we should** ☐. 우리가 ~해야 한다고 생각합니다.

① be proud of our performance
② reform our pay system to reduce the tax burden
③ invest in upgrading the production facilities
▶ 우리의 성과를 자랑스러워 해야 / 세금 부담을 줄이기 위해 급여 시스템을 개선해야 / 생산 설비를 업그레이드하는 데 투자해야

3　**Could we hear from** ☐? ~의 의견을 들어볼 수 있을까요?

① Bob from the Accounting Department
② Howard, who is in charge of international marketing
③ Richard from the Personnel Department
▶ 회계부의 밥 / 국제 마케팅을 담당하고 있는 하워드 / 인사부의 리처드

06.mp3

A [1]**In my opinion**, we need to adjust our overtime system.

B What do you mean?

A Right now, we all email our overtime hours to the Personnel Department daily.

B [2]**What's wrong with** that?

A This makes it too difficult for the personnel workers to process the information.

B So what's your suggestion?

A [3]**I recommend** emailing the overtime hours on a monthly basis. That way, they would have enough time to process the information without making any errors.

B That sounds like a good idea.

Pattern Training

1 **In my opinion,** [_____]. 제 생각에는, ~.

① business expansion is necessary
② we should handle this customer complaint first
③ you should come up with a new idea for a radio advertisement

▶ 사업 확장이 필수적입니다 / 우선 이 고객 불만을 처리해야 합니다 / 라디오 광고를 위한 새로운 아이디어를 생각해내야 합니다

2 **What's wrong with** [_____]? ~에 뭐가 문제죠?

① our marketing campaign
② my report
③ celebrating his retirement

▶ 우리의 마케팅 캠페인 / 제 보고서 / 그의 은퇴를 축하하는 것

3 **I recommend** [_____]. ~을 제안합니다.

① concentrating on our domestic market
② that we attend the three-day workshop
③ postponing our meeting until he comes back from his vacation

▶ 국내 시장에 집중할 것 / 우리가 3일간의 워크숍에 참석할 것 / 그가 휴가에서 돌아올 때까지 회의를 연기할 것

A Make sentences using the given words.

| my point / take over | obvious / be superior to |
| suggest / offer / sales staff | seem / room for cooperation |

1 제게는 두 회사 간에 서로 협력할 여지가 있어 보입니다.

▶ _____

2 우리 근로자들이 다른 근로자들보다 우수하다는 것은 확실합니다.

▶ _____

3 제 요지는 아무도 그 사람 자리를 대신하고 싶어하지 않는다는 것입니다.

▶ _____

4 영업 사원들에게 인센티브 제도를 제공하는 것을 제안합니다.

▶ _____

B Choose the best expression for each blank.

| ⓐ Could we hear | ⓑ What I was trying to say |
| ⓒ one of the best ways | ⓓ Speaking of |

1

A: So, what you're saying is we need to develop another product?

B: No. _____ is that we must do market research first before we develop a product.

그러니까 당신 말은 우리가 다른 상품을 개발할 필요가 있다는 건가요? – 아뇨. 제가 말하고자 했던 바는 상품을 개발하기 전에 먼저 시장 조사를 해야 한다는 것입니다.

2

A: Let's begin with the first agenda item. It's about protecting the rights of our workers. _____ from Mr. Johnson on that?

B: Sure. _____ workers' rights, we need to accept their requests.

첫 번째 안건부터 시작합시다. 근로자의 권리 보호에 관한 것입니다. 거기에 대해 존슨 씨의 의견을 들어볼 수 있을까요? – 그럼요. 근로자의 권리에 대해 말하자면, 우리는 그들의 요구를 받아들여야 합니다.

3

A: Richard, I know that you've prepared a report on how to market our products effectively. Please tell us about it briefly.

B: I think _____ is to sponsor Hollywood movies.

리처드, 당신이 우리 제품을 효과적으로 시장에 내놓는 법에 대한 보고서를 준비했다고 알고 있습니다. 우리에게 그것에 대해 간략히 이야기해주시죠. – 제 생각에 좋은 방법 중 하나는 할리우드 영화를 후원하는 것입니다.

Practice 2 · Listen-up!

A Listen to the dialog and check true or false.

07.mp3

	True	False
1 The second item on the agenda is about a weekly report.		
2 Their project is due in two months.		
3 They are likely to put an ad in the paper to find more workers.		

B Listen again and complete the blanks.

07.mp3

Manager: Let's __1_____ _____ _____ the second item. It's about our bridge construction project. __2_____ _____ the weekly progress report, I found that it's still in its infancy. Did you know that? The deadline for the project is __3_____ _____ _____ just two months.

Robert: __4_____ _____ _____, we should hire more workers to complete it on time.

Manager: Do you have __5_____ _____ that would help us find more engineers as soon as possible?

Robert: __6_____ _____ that we put a want ad in the local paper.

Manager: I think that's a good idea.

C Listen to the dialog and answer the questions.

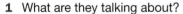

08.mp3

1 What are they talking about?

2 How many people can the gym accommodate at once?

3 What is the problem with the gym?

4 What is Mr. Walker concerned about?

+ BIZ TIPs   효과적으로 회의하는 법

직원들과 정기적인 회의(regular meeting)를 갖는 것은 회사 발전에 있어서 아주 중요하다. 그러나 효과적인 회의(effective meeting)를 하기란 쉽지 않다. 이를 위해 다음 사항을 반드시 기억해두자.

▷ **Define your agenda. 안건을 정의하라**
안건을 확실히 정하고 그 이외의 것은 논의 대상에서 제외한다.

▷ **Make handouts of your agenda. 안건을 인쇄물로 만들어라**
논의 사항을 미리 복사해서 참석자들에게 나눠준다.

▷ **Take down the minutes of the meeting.**
회의의 세부사항을 적어둬라
회의에서 나온 의견은 모두 메모해 두어야 후속 조치가 가능하다.

▷ **Don't forget to follow up. 회의 후 진행 상황을 항상 주시하라**
회의에서는 향후의 행동 방향이 정해진다. 회의 후에 어떻게 일이 진행되는지 반드시 파악하라.

회의 통제하기 및 끝맺기

Controlling and Wrapping up a Meeting

Vocabulary & Expressions

끼어들기 및 통제하기

- **interrupt** 끼어들다, 가로막다
- **I'm sorry to interrupt, but** 끼어들어서 죄송하지만,
- **add A to B** A를 B에 추가하다
- **wait until** ~까지 기다리다
- **finish one's point** ~의 논점을 마저 끝마치다
- **go on to** ~으로 넘어가다 (= move on to, turn to)

- **get off the point** 요지에서 벗어나다 (= get side-tracked)
- **return to the main issue** 주요 논점사항으로 돌아가다
- **be short of time** 시간이 부족하다 (= run out of time)
- **speak one by one** 한 명씩 말하다
- **skip** 건너뛰다 (= pass over)
- **postpone** 미루다

결론 정리하고 끝맺기

- **summarize** ~을 요약하다 (= sum up, recap)
- **reach a conclusion** 결론에 이르다 (reach = come to)
- **common ground** 타협점
- **We have decided to** 우리는 ~하기로 결정하였습니다
- **It seems that we're all agreed that**
  우리 모두 ~에 동의한 것 같군요

- **To summarize our discussion,** 우리의 회의 내용을 요약하자면,
- **arrange a date for the next meeting** 다음 회의 일정을 잡다
- **list the action items** 행동 지침을 목록으로 작성하다
- **cover everything on the agenda**
  안건사항을 모두 다루다[끝마치다]

끝맺는 인사말

- **We've made some good progress today.** 오늘 상당한 진전이 있었습니다.
- **Thank you for coming and for your contributions.** 오셔서 기여해주신 데에 감사 드립니다.

Useful Expressions

Let me summarize the main points.	주요 사항들을 요약하도록 하겠습니다.
Can we go on to the next topic?	계속해서 다음 주제로 넘어갈까요?
We are running out of time.	시간이 없습니다.
What we have agreed upon is to renew our contract.	우리가 합의를 본 것은 우리의 계약을 갱신하는 겁니다.
To sum up, it's a breach of our contract.	요약하면, 그것은 계약 위반입니다.

Vocabulary Check-Up

A Match the meanings on the left with the expressions on the right.

1 타협점 ·   · ⓐ progress

2 논지에서 벗어난 ·   · ⓑ common ground

3 상기시키는 메모나 메일 ·   · ⓒ attendee

4 진전, 진척 ·   · ⓓ off the point

5 참석자, 출석자 ·   · ⓔ reminder

B Fill in the blanks using the given words.

1 오늘 회의는 아주 알찼습니다.
   ▶ Today's meeting was very _____.

2 끼어들어서 죄송합니다만, 질문 하나 해도 될까요?
   ▶ Sorry to _____, but can I ask you a question?

3 회사 정책을 조정할 필요가 있다는 점에 우리는 기본적으로 동의했습니다.
   ▶ We _____ agreed that we need to adjust our company policy.

4 우리는 중국에 공장을 열기로 결정했습니다.
   ▶ We have _____ to open the plant in China.

5 안건을 모두 다룬 것 같군요.
   ▶ I think we've _____ everything on the agenda.

Words
basically
cover
interrupt
fruitful
decide

C Refer to the Korean and fill in the blanks.

1 Please list the _____ _____ each of the participants is responsible for.
   참가자 각자가 취해야 할 행동 지침을 목록으로 작성해주세요.

2 We _____ _____ _____ about the size of the training center.
   우리는 훈련센터의 규모에 대한 결론에 이르렀습니다.

3 Please let me _____ _____ _____ before we move on to the next topic.
   다음 주제로 넘어가기 전에 제 논점을 끝마치도록 해주세요.

4 Let's _____ to the issue of our marketing budget.
   우리의 마케팅 예산 문제로 다시 돌아갑시다.

5 Let me _____ today's meeting.
   오늘 회의를 요약하도록 하겠습니다.

09.mp3

A Excuse me. May I interrupt you for a moment?

B Sure, go ahead.

A I think we should have a branch in China to win back our market share.

B Sophia, you seem to be getting off the point. That's not on the agenda.

A I'm sorry. But ¹**please let me finish** my point.

B Why don't we leave that for the next meeting?

A Okay. No problem.

B ²**Can we go on to discuss** the third agenda item?

C Yes, I believe that ³**we should take** Saturdays **off** to boost our employees' morale.

B Oh, I'm afraid we are running out of time. Can you make your point in two minutes?

Pattern Training

1   Please let me finish _____. ~을 끝마치게 해주세요.

① my speech
② my question
③ what I was about to say

▶ 제 강연 / 제 질문 / 제가 말하고자 했던 것

2   Can we go on to discuss _____? 계속해서 ~을 논의할까요?

① marketing costs
② the issue of working conditions
③ the vision of our company

▶ 마케팅 비용 / 근무 환경 문제 / 우리 회사의 비전

3   We should take _____ **off.** ~에 일하지 않고 쉬어야 합니다.

① tomorrow
② our company's birthday
③ the presidential election day

▶ 내일 / 회사 창립일 / 대통령 선거일

10.mp3

A Olivia, **¹could you summarize** what we've agreed on?

B Of course. **²We basically agreed that** we would continue to outsource the product.

A I'd like you to email us a meeting summary by the end of this week.

B No problem, sir.

A Is there anything more to discuss?

C No. I think we've covered all the issues.

A All right. Let's stop here since time is up. We made very good progress today.

D **³Aren't we supposed to** have another meeting?

A Yeah, I will send a reminder to all of the attendees two days before the meeting date. Thank you for your participation.

Pattern Training

1 **Could you summarize** [_____]**?** ~을 요약해주실래요?

① this report
② what we've been talking about so far
③ in your own words what Howard said

▶ 이 보고서 / 지금까지 우리가 이야기한 것 / 당신의 방식으로 하워드가 말한 것

2 **We basically agreed that** [_____]**.**

기본적으로 우리는 ~에 합의했습니다.

① we should put off the meeting
② the contract must be amended
③ we should be able to produce 1,000 units a day

▶ 회의를 연기해야 한다는 것 / 계약서가 수정되어야 한다는 것 / 하루에 1천 개를 생산할 수 있어야 한다는 것

📄 유사 표현

▸ **What we've agreed upon is that** an initial one-year contract would be enough for us to start the business.

우리가 동의한 것은 초기 일년 계약 정도면 우리가 사업을 시작하기에 충분하다는 것**입니다.**

3 **Aren't we supposed to** [_____]**?** ~하기로 되어 있지 않았나요?

① have a meeting at 6
② take a ten-minute break
③ discuss the training curriculum

▶ 6시에 회의를 하기로 / 10분간 휴식을 취하기로 / 훈련 커리큘럼을 논의하기로

A Make sentences using the given words.

interrupt / ask a question	seem / get off	have decided to / offer
sum up / make a decision	make / good progress	go on / second issue

1 오늘 상당한 진전이 있었습니다.　　　　　　　　　▶ We _____

2 당신의 말은 논지에서 벗어난 것 같군요.　　　　　　▶ You _____

3 우리는 8월 동안 고객들에게 10% 할인 쿠폰을 제공하기로 결정했습니다.　▶ We _____

4 계속해서 두 번째 주제를 논의할까요?　　　　　　　▶ Can _____

5 우리가 내린 결정사항들을 요약해주시겠어요?　　　▶ Could _____

6 끼어들어서 정말 죄송한데요, 질문 하나 해도 될까요?　▶ I'm _____

B Put the Korean into English and complete the dialogs.

1

A: 한 사람씩 말씀해주세요. (one by one)

B: Okay. I'll wait until he finishes his point.

2

A: Then, let's go on to the next issue.

B: I'm afraid we're rather short of time.

　세 번째 안건은 다음 회의로 미루는 게 어때요? (Why don't we / postpone)

3

A: Let's stop here since time is up.

B: Jane, could you summarize what we have agreed on?

A: 토의 내용을 요약하자면, 더 많은 고객을 끌기 위해 우리는 웹사이트를 만들 것입니다.

　(To sum up / build a website)

4

A: 드디어 결론에 도달한 것 같군요. (I think / conclusion)

B: It has been a very useful discussion.

A: No doubt about it. I think we can end the meeting now.

　참석해주셔서 감사합니다. (Thanks for)

A   Listen to the dialog and answer the questions.   11.mp3

1   What is the main issue that the speakers are talking about?

▶

2   What is Lisa talking about?

▶

3   How many agenda items have they discussed so far?

▶

B   Listen again and complete the blanks.   11.mp3

Lisa: ___¹___ _____ _____ you for a moment?

Manager: Sure, go ahead.

Lisa: ___²___ _____ _____ 50% off the prices of all items during the summer sale.

Manager: Lisa, you seem to be ___³_____ _____ _____ _____. We're not talking about the prices but about the quality of our products.

Lisa: Oh, I'm sorry. But please let me ___⁴___ _____ _____.

Manager: Sorry, but we should just ___⁵___ _____ _____ _____ _____ only.

Lisa: Okay.

Manager: ___⁶___ _____ _____ _____ the third agenda item.

C   Listen to the dialog and check true or false.   12.mp3

	True	False
1 Allan agreed that he will write and share a copy of the minutes.		
2 The speakers are satisfied with the result of the meeting.		
3 The date for the next meeting is tomorrow.		
4 Some issues haven't been covered yet.		

동의하기 및 반대하기

Agreeing and Disagreeing

Vocabulary & Expressions

동의하기

- **I agree with *someone*** ~의 의견에 동의합니다.
- **I agree to that.** 그 점에 동의합니다.
- **I'm in complete agreement. / I agree entirely.** 전적으로 동의합니다.
- **That's a great idea.** 아주 좋은 생각입니다.
- **That's a very valuable point.** 아주 좋은 지적입니다.
- **You can say that again.** 지당한 말씀입니다.

반대하기

- **I don't agree with you.** 당신 의견에 동의하지 않습니다.
- **I'm against that because** ~이기 때문에 저는 거기에 반대합니다
- **I'm afraid that I don't think so.** 죄송하지만 저는 그렇게 생각하지 않습니다.
- **I disagree completely.** 저는 전적으로 반대합니다.
- **I'm not comfortable with your idea.** 당신 생각에 동의할 수가 없네요.

부분적으로 동의하기

- **I partly agree to that, but** 그 점에 일부 동의지만.
- **That may be right, but** 맞는 말씀일지도 모르지만.
- **I see what you're saying, but** 무슨 말씀인지 이해하지만.

간략히 요점 말하기

- **In short, / In brief, / In a nutshell, / To make a long story short,** 간략히 말하면.
- **In other words,** 다시 말하면
- **My message[meaning] is** 제가 하고자 하는 말은 ~입니다

의견 강조하기

- **Let me emphasize that** ~을 강조하고자 합니다
- **I'd like to point out that** ~을 지적하고 싶습니다
- **The point I'd like to stress is that** 제가 강조하고자 하는 점은 ~라는 것입니다
- **What we need to do is to** 우리가 해야 할 일은 ~하는 것입니다
- **We see no alternative but to** ~하는 수밖에 없습니다 (= We have no choice but to)

Useful Expressions

- I partly agree to that opinion.
  그 의견에 **일부 동의합니다.**
- Keep in mind that we are all in the same boat.
  우리 모두 같은 배를 탄 운명이**라는 점을 명심하십시오.**
- In a nutshell, we should scratch the plan.
  간략히 말하면, 우리는 그 계획을 취소해야 합니다.
- I believe that's the way we can survive.
  그것이 우리가 생존할 수 있는 **길이라고** 믿습니다.
- We see no alternative but to withdraw from the market.
  그 시장에서 철수하는 **수밖에 없습니다.**

Vocabulary Check-Up

A Match the meanings on the left with the expressions on the right.

1 시장 크기 ·   · ⓐ competitor

2 현재의 경향 ·   · ⓑ market size

3 경쟁자 ·   · ⓒ proposal

4 제안, 건의 ·   · ⓓ marketing strategy

5 마케팅 전략 ·   · ⓔ current trend

B Fill in the blanks with the given words.

Words
point out
emphasize
my meaning
agree with
against

1 우리의 공급업체들이 못 미덥다는 당신의 의견에 동의합니다.
▶ I _____ _____ you in that our vendors are not reliable.

2 우리가 낭비할 돈이 없다는 것을 지적하고 싶습니다.
▶ I'd like to _____ _____ that we don't have any money to burn.

3 저는 당신 제안에 반대합니다.
▶ I'm _____ your suggestions.

4 제 말은 당신의 주장 대부분이 이치에 맞지 않는다는 것입니다.
▶ _____ _____ is that most of your arguments do not hold water.

5 오로지 숫자에만 중점을 둘 때가 아니라는 것을 강조하고 싶습니다.
▶ Let me _____ that this is not a time to focus solely on numbers.

C Refer to the Korean and fill in the blanks.

1 I _____ _____ you're saying, but I don't think we have to bid for the project.
무슨 말씀인지는 알지만, 그 프로젝트에 입찰할 필요는 없다고 생각합니다.

2 _____ _____ words, her background doesn't fit this position.
다시 말하면, 그녀의 경력은 이 자리에 맞지 않아요.

3 I _____ with some of your suggestions.
당신의 일부 제안에 반대합니다.

4 _____ we need to _____ is to encourage shoppers to browse our merchandise.
우리가 해야 할 일은 쇼핑객들이 우리 상품을 둘러보도록 부추기는 것입니다.

5 _____ _____ a long story _____, we must win back our market share.
간략히 말하면, 우리의 시장점유율을 다시 되찾아야 합니다.

13.mp3

A Our sales in the States have been dropping over the last five years. So we see no choice but to amend our marketing strategy.

B ¹**I partly agree** to that, but you should keep in mind that the market size has shrunk.

A ²**I'm afraid that** I don't think so. Please take a look at the data released by DataResearch. It's still growing.

B Are you sure?

A Yeah, it has grown 30% since 2016.

B I thought it was decreasing. But I was wrong. Thank you for your input.

A ³**We should do something to** turn things around.

Pattern Training

1 **I partly agree that** [_____]. ~에 일부 동의합니다.

① the documentation is not clear
② this product is very poorly designed
③ our efforts to date have not lived up to their expectations

▶ 문서가 명확하지 않다는 것 / 이 제품이 형편없이 설계되었다는 것 / 현재까지 우리의 노력이 그들의 기대에 못 미친다는 것

🔘 동의를 나타내는 표현

▸ Absolutely. 당연하죠.
▸ Exactly. 바로 그겁니다.
▸ Sure. 물론이죠.
▸ Impressive. 인상적이네요.
▸ Excellent. 훌륭해요.
▸ Definitely. 당연하죠.
▸ You said it. 맞습니다.

2 **I'm afraid that** [_____]. 유감스럽지만 ~입니다.

① I can't do that
② I can't accept your proposal
③ we need to make any decisive decision right here

▶ 저는 그것을 할 수 없습니다 / 당신의 제안을 받아들일 수 없습니다 / 지금 당장 과감한 결정을 내려야 합니다

3 **We should do something to** [_____]. ~하기 위해 무언가를 해야 합니다.

① co-operate with our competitors
② make our company profitable
③ find a solution to this problem

▶ 경쟁자와 협력하기 / 회사가 수익이 나도록 하기 / 이 문제에 대한 해결책을 찾기

14.mp3

A **¹I'd like to point out that** our competitors are producing smaller items.

B You can say that again. That's the trend these days, I guess.

A The KDT Company just released a new product which is smaller than the previous model.

B How's it doing on the market?

A It's been well received so far.

B **²We see no alternative but to** follow the current trend. What do you think?

A Well, I think we need to differentiate our products from others on the market.

B Please fill me in.

A **³In a nutshell**, we make ours bigger rather than smaller. I believe that's the way we can survive.

Pattern Training

1 **I'd like to point out that** ┊＿＿＿＿＿＿＿┊. ~라는 점을 지적하고 싶습니다.

① we should develop a better benefits package
② it's hard to predict what the result will be
③ we are talking about a multi-million dollar contract

▶ 더 나은 복리후생 제도를 개발해야 한다는 / 결과가 어떨지 예측하기 어렵다는 / 우리가 수백만 달러짜리 계약에 대해 얘기하고 있다는

2 **We see no alternative but to** ┊＿＿＿＿＿＿＿┊.
~하는 수밖에 없습니다.

① recruit workers from overseas
② delete the files on his personal computer
③ make copycat products

▶ 해외에서 직원을 고용하는 / 그의 개인 컴퓨터에 있는 파일들을 지우는 / 모방 제품을 만드는

🔵 반대를 나타내는 표현

· Nonsense. 말도 안 돼요.
· It doesn't make sense.
  논리에 안 맞아요.
· That's unthinkable.
  그건 생각조차 할 수 없어요.
· Wake up! 정신 차리세요!
· Horrible. / Terrible. 형편없군요.

3 **In a nutshell,** ┊＿＿＿＿＿＿＿┊. 간단히 말하면, ~.

① I value the effort he puts into his work
② it's really not that hard to learn how to operate the system
③ we need more workers to finish the project by the end of the month

▶ 그가 일에 쏟는 노력을 높이 평가합니다 / 그 시스템 작동법을 배우는 것은 그리 어렵지 않습니다 / 월말까지 그 프로젝트를 끝내려면 더 많은 직원이 필요합니다

Practice 1 | Let's Speak!

A Find the correct responses to complete the dialogs.

1 What do you mean?

2 We have no choice but to switch delivery companies.

3 Let me emphasize that he is not the right person for the project.

4 We need to cut back on our budget.

5 I would like to point out that we must meet the deadline for submitting our proposal.

> **Responses**
> ⓐ In brief, he is dragging his heels on the project.
> ⓑ How can we possibly meet the deadline without working overtime?
> ⓒ That may be right, but who else in our group can lead the project?
> ⓓ What's wrong with our delivery company?
> ⓔ I'm against that because we are planning to make a TV commercial.

B Make sentences using the given words.

point out / a face-to-face meeting the way / compete against	in other words / look like partly agree / change	keep in mind / control be afraid / think

1 그것이 우리가 경쟁사들과 경쟁할 수 있는 방법입니다.

▶ _____

2 달리 말하자면, 우리 회사가 외부에서 어떻게 보이는지를 고려해야 합니다.

▶ _____

3 유감이지만 저는 그렇게 생각하지 않습니다.

▶ _____

4 고객들이 어떻게 반응할지 통제할 수는 없다는 것을 명심하세요.

▶ _____

5 그 점에는 부분적으로 동의하지만 우리의 계획을 변경할 수는 없어요.

▶ _____

6 그들과 직접 만나서 회의를 해야 할 필요가 있다는 점을 지적하고 싶습니다.

▶ _____

A Listen to the dialog and answer the questions.

15.mp3

1 What are they talking about?

▶ ....

2 What is the problem with the current vendor?

▶ ....

3 What does Peter like about the current vendor?

▶ ....

4 What is Emily worried about?

▶ ....

B Listen again and complete the blanks.

15.mp3

Emily: Peter, ¹_____ _____ _____, we should switch CPU vendors.

Peter: ² _____ _____ _____?

Emily: Because our current vendor is charging us too much.

Peter: I ³ _____ _____ _____ _____, Emily. But money is not everything.

Emily: I'd like to point out that we can lower our product prices if we use other CPUs.

Peter: I'm ⁴ _____ _____ _____ your idea. Please ⁵ _____ _____ _____

that they are second to none when it comes to product quality.

Emily: I know their CPUs are reliable, Peter. However, if we keep using their CPUs, we will

⁶ _____ _____ _____ _____.

C Listen to the dialog and check true or false.

16.mp3

	True	False
1 AIZ is dominating the market.		
2 Richard thinks they should reduce the advertising budget.		
3 Sarah will leave the meeting earlier.		
4 AIZ spent a lot of money on advertising.		

Larry King
"King of Debates"

When he was a young man, Larry King [1]**hopped on** a bus for the Southeast, where a media market [2]**was in the midst of** [3]**blossoming**. His life-long dream was to become a broadcaster.

However, it was not easy. After encountering several obstacles, he finally got his first radio gig as a DJ in Miami for WIOD-Radio, and, in 1960, he entered the realm of television [4]**for the first time**.

When King was chosen to [5]**host** a nationally televised live show entitled The Larry King Show, he finally became a national [6]**figure**.

In 1983, King was offered a shot on national television when Post-Newsweek distributed a syndicated show to 118 stations with King as host. While the show did not succeed, it did catch the eye of media mogul Ted Turner, who took King to the then-fledgling Cable News Network, CNN.

King was later inducted into the Broadcasting Hall of Fame of Broadcasting Magazine and the National Association of Broadcasters.

© photo.ua/shutterstock

© Kathy Hutchins/shutterstock

래리 킹은 젊었을 때 미국 남동부 지방으로 가는 버스에 올라탔다. 그곳에서는 미디어 시장이 한창 붐을 맞고 있었다. 그의 평생의 꿈은 방송인이 되는 것이었다.

하지만 그것은 쉽지 않았다. 몇 번의 역경을 만난 후에 그는 마침내 마이애미에서 WIOD 라디오 디제이로 쇼를 맡게 되었다. 그리고 1960년에 그는 처음으로 TV계에 입성했다.

그가 '래리 킹 쇼'라는 제목의 전국으로 방영되는 생방송 사회자가 되면서 그는 전국구 인물이 되었다.

1983년, 그는 Post-Newsweek가 118개 방송국으로 유통시키는 전국 방송 쇼의 진행자 기회를 얻게 되었다. 그 쇼는 성공하지 못했지만, 미디어의 황제 테드 터너의 눈을 사로잡았다. 그는 킹을 당시 신생 케이블 뉴스 네트워크인 CNN으로 데려갔다.

킹은 나중에 Broadcasting Magazine과 전미방송협회의 방송 명예의 전당에 헌액되었다.

© Hayk_Shalunts/
shutterstock

© Anton_Ivanov/shutterstock

1 hop on ~에 뛰어오르다

He **hopped on** a shuttle bus in the rain to get to the airport.
그는 공항으로 가려고 빗속에서 버스에 올라탔다.

2 be in the midst of ~하는 중이다

▶ in the middle of와 비슷한 의미.

We **are in the midst of** revising our strategy for international operations.
저희는 지금 해외 운영 전략을 다시 검토하는 중입니다.

3 blossom 피어나다, 번영하다

▶ 꽃 등이 피어나는 것을 의미하는데, 굳이 꽃이 아니더라도 비유적인 표현으로 많이 쓰인다.

Only time will tell if our business will **blossom**.
우리 사업이 번창할지는 오직 시간만이 말해줄 겁니다.

4 for the first time 처음으로

For the first time, our company made a profit!
우리 회사가 처음으로 수익을 냈습니다!

5 host (TV프로의) 사회를 보다, (행사를) 주최하다

▶ host는 그 자체가 명사로 '사회자'라는 뜻도 있다.

Who's supposed to **host** the meeting?
누가 그 회의를 주최하기로 되어 있나요?

6 figure 유명한 인물

▶ famous person이라고 바꾸어 쓸 수 있다.

The movement is supported by key **figures** in the organization.
그 운동은 조직의 주요 인물들에게 지원받고 있습니다.

Who is Larry King?

본명은 Lawrence Harvey Ziegler로, 1933년 11월 19일 뉴욕 브루클린에서 태어났다. 러시아 피가 흐르는 그의 아버지는 식당을 운영하다가 래리가 11살 때 사망했다. 그의 어머니는 자식을 부양하기 위해 지원을 받아야 할 만큼 가난했다. 그는 가난했지만 끝없는 의지로 지금의 자리에 오르게 되었다. CNN에서 토크쇼인 Larry King Live를 무려 25년 동안 진행하며 정치인, 기업인 등 수많은 유명인사들과 인터뷰를 했고 큰 인기를 끌었다.

© Tinseltown/shutterstock

Larry King says...

"I remind myself every morning: Nothing I say this day will teach me anything. So if I'm going to learn, I must do it by listening."
아침마다 난 자신에게 일깨운다. 오늘 내가 하는 말은 내게 아무런 교훈을 남기지 않을 것이다. 따라서 내가 배우려면, 들어야 한다.

"I fantasized being a broadcaster."
나는 방송인이 되는 걸 상상했다.

"If you do something, expect consequences."
당신이 어떤 일을 하려고 한다면, 결과를 예상하며 하라.

Practical Business
Business Presentations

PART 2
비즈니스 프레젠테이션

WEEK 04

발표 목적과 발표자 소개

Introducing the Goal of the Presentation and the Presenter

Vocabulary & Expressions

발표자 소개하기

- I've been working in this field for ~동안 이 분야에서 일하고 있습니다
- I have ... of experience in this field. 저는 이 분야에서 ~의 경력이 있습니다.
- I'm working as + 신분/직위. ~으로서 일하고 있습니다.
- I'm in charge of / I'm responsible for 저는 ~을 맡고 있습니다

발표 주제 및 목적 말하기

- The title[subject] of my presentation is 제 발표의 제목[주제]는 ~입니다
- Today, I'm going to present about 오늘 ~에 대해 발표하려고 합니다
- What I'd like to talk about is 제가 얘기하고자 하는 것은 ~에 대한 겁니다
- I'm going to update you on ~에 대한 최신 정보를 알려드리겠습니다
- The purpose[objective] of my presentation is 제 발표의 목적은 ~입니다

발표 절차 소개하기

- I'll begin by giving you a brief outline of
  ~에 대한 개요를 간략히 전달하는 것으로 시작하겠습니다 (outline 개요, ~의 개요를 서술하다)
- My presentation is broken down into /
  My presentation is divided into 제 발표는 ~부분으로 나뉩니다
- take a look at ~을 살펴보다 (= examine)
- feel free to 자유롭게 ~하다

Plus Tip

일반적인 발표 순서

1. 청중 환영하기
2. 본인 소개하기
3. 발표 주제 소개하기
4. 발표 절차 알리기
5. 본격적인 발표 시작하기
6. 결론 맺기
7. 요약하기
8. 질문 받기

발표 순서 말하기

- First, 우선, 먼저
- Second, 둘째
- Third, 셋째
- Finally, 마지막으로
- Lastly, 마지막으로

- Firstly, 첫째로
- Secondly, 둘째로
- Then[Next], 그런 다음
- After that, 그 후에

Useful Expressions

- Thank you for taking time off from your busy schedule to be with us. 바쁘신 중에도 시간을 내 저희와 함께해주셔서 **감사합니다.**
- I've been working in this field for 3 years. **저는 이 분야에서** 3년간 **일하고 있습니다.**
- My goal is to make a top-notch product. **제 목표는** 최고의 제품을 만드**는 것입니다.**
- I'd like to introduce Mr. Howard Cha. 하워드 차 씨를 **소개합니다.**
- My presentation will take around 30 minutes. **제 발표는** 30분 가량 **걸릴 겁니다.**

Vocabulary Check-Up

A Match the meanings on the left with the expressions on the right.

1 박사 학위　·
2 시장 점유율　·
3 광고 전략　·
4 시간을 내다　·
5 박수갈채　·

· ⓐ market share
· ⓑ doctorate
· ⓒ applause
· ⓓ advertising strategies
· ⓔ take time off

B Fill in the blanks using the given words.

1 이 업계의 최신 기술에 대해 얘기하려고 합니다.
▶ I'm going to _____ _____ the latest technology in this industry.

2 오늘 우리는 전자상거래의 영향력을 면밀히 살펴볼 것입니다.
▶ Today, we're going to _____ the power of e-commerce.

3 제 발표는 네 가지 주요 부분으로 나뉩니다.
▶ My presentation _____ _____ into four main sections.

4 마지막으로, 우리 제품 범위를 어떻게 다양화할지 논의하고 싶습니다.
▶ _____, I'd like to discuss how to diversify our product range.

5 그 후에, 우리의 매출을 나타낸 차트 몇 개를 보여드릴 것입니다.
▶ _____ _____, I'm going to show you some charts illustrating our sales.

> **Words**
> after that
> finally
> talk about
> examine
> divide

C Refer to the Korean and fill in the blanks.

1 First, I'd like to _____ my presentation before I start.
먼저, 본격적으로 시작하기 전에 제 발표의 개요를 말씀 드리겠습니다.

2 We're going to _____ _____ _____ at the results of our customer survey.
고객 설문조사 결과를 살펴볼 것입니다.

3 I'm Mark Evans, and my position is in the _____ _____.
저는 마크 이반으로 영업부에서 근무하고 있습니다.

4 I'd be grateful if you could _____ me your questions _____ the 10-minute break.
10분의 휴식 시간 동안 질문을 해주시면 감사하겠습니다.

5 The _____ of this presentation is to educate you about the present market conditions.
이 발표의 목적은 현재의 시장 상황에 대해 여러분들을 교육하는 것입니다.

17.mp3

[1]**Thank you for** taking time off from your busy schedule to be with us.

I've asked you to be here because [2]**I would like to introduce** Mr. Howard Cha. Howard has been hired as our new project consultant.

He has over 23 years of experience in this field. For the last 10 years, he worked for a company called ThreeStar. Howard is a Project Management Professional member and has a doctorate from Drexel University in Philadelphia.

And now [3]**he is going to talk about** how to manage a project efficiently. Let's all give a big round of applause to Mr. Howard Cha.

Pattern Training

1 **Thank you for** [_____]. ~에 대해 감사 드립니다.

① your time

② meeting with me after working hours

③ coming to the MCM Award Ceremony

▶ 시간을 내주신 데 / 근무 시간 후에 저를 만나주신 데 / MCM 시상식에 와주신 데

More Expressions

발표 시작 전의 첫 인사

▸ I'm honored to be with you.
여러분과 함께하게 되어 영광입니다.

▸ I'm pleased to be with you tonight.
오늘밤 여러분과 함께하게 되어 기쁩니다.

2 **I would like to introduce** [_____]. ~를 소개하고자 합니다.

① an award winner

② our senior vice president

③ Ms. Helen Clark who has more than 13 years of experience in this industry

▶ 수상자 / 우리의 수석 부사장 / 이 업계에서 13년 이상의 경력이 있는 헬렌 클락 씨

3 **He is going to talk about** [_____]. ~에 대해서 말씀 드릴 것입니다.

① the future of this company

② his goals for the marketing team

③ the importance of worker health care

▶ 이 회사의 미래 / 마케팅 팀에 대한 그의 목표 / 근로자 건강 관리의 중요성

18.mp3

Hello, everyone.

As you all know, we are losing our market share in India. But we can't sit around doing nothing about that. [1]**My goal is to** increase it by 10 to 20% within two years. How can we possibly increase it in a shrinking market? The subject of my presentation today is how we can do this.

[2]**My presentation is divided into** three main sections. Firstly, I am going to look at the current market situation. And then I am going to talk to you about our products and how they fit in. Finally, I'm going to examine some advertising strategies.

[3]**The presentation will take** around 30 minutes. I'd be grateful if you could ask me your questions after the presentation.

Pattern Training

1 **My goal is to** [_____]. 저의 목표는 ~하는 것입니다.

① become a project manager
② make my company profitable
③ fight my competitors and come out on top

▶ 프로젝트 매니저가 되는 / 회사가 이윤이 나도록 만드는 / 경쟁사와 싸워서 최고가 되는

2 **My presentation is divided into** [_____].
저의 발표는 ~으로 나뉩니다.

① two major sections
② three major topics
③ four parts with a brief introduction

▶ 두 가지 주요 부문 / 세 가지 주요 주제 / 간략한 소개와 함께 네 가지 부문

○ 유사 표현

My presentation is in five parts.
제 발표는 다섯 부분으로 되어 있습니다.
My presentation consists of the following parts.
제 발표는 다음과 같은 부분으로 구성됩니다.

3 **The presentation will take** [_____]. 발표는 ~ (시간이) 걸릴 것입니다.

① 20 minutes
② about an hour and a half
③ approximately 30 minutes

▶ 20분 / 약 한 시간 반 / 대략 30분

Practice 1   Let's Speak!

A   Make sentences using the given words.

purpose / sick leave	take / around	be divided into / sections
update / features	have experience / industry	thank you for / take time off

1 바쁘신 와중에도 이렇게 시간을 내 자리해주셔서 감사합니다.

  ▶ _____

2 우리의 신제품의 가장 중요한 특징들에 대해 최신 정보를 알려드리고자 합니다.

  ▶ I'm going to _____

3 제 발표의 목적은 병가에 관한 회사 정책을 논의하는 것입니다.

  ▶ _____

4 제 발표는 세 부분으로 나뉩니다.

  ▶ _____

5 제 발표는 20분 정도 걸릴 겁니다.

  ▶ _____

6 그는 이 업계에서 12년 이상의 경력이 있습니다.

  ▶ _____

B   Fill in the blanks with the given words.

1 I'm in charge of the Special Project Team.

= I'm _____ for the Special Project Team.

2 Please do not hesitate to ask any questions.

= _____ you have any questions, feel _____ to ask them.

3 I have 7 years of experience in this area.

= I've been _____ in this _____ for 7 years.

4 I plan to speak for about 20 minutes.

= My presentation will _____ around 20 minutes.

5 I'm the financial analyst for BK Associates.

= I am working for BK Associates, _____ a financial analyst.

6 What I'm going to talk about today is our business expansion plan.

= The _____ of my presentation is our business expansion plan.

Words
take
if
as
subject
free
responsible
working
field

A   Listen to the presentation and answer the questions.   19.mp3

1   What field is Dr. Klein working in?

▶

2   How many books has he published until now?

▶

3   What kind of degree does he have?

▶

4   What is he going to talk about?

▶

B   Listen to the presentation and check true or false.   20.mp3

	True	False
1 The speaker is talking about the GRE exam.		
2 The presentation consists of three sections.		
3 The presentation will take 40 minutes.		
4 The audience can ask questions at any time.		

C   Listen again and complete the blanks.   20.mp3

Hello, folks! Thank you __¹_____ _____ _____ . __²_____ _____ of my presentation this evening is how to score well on the TOEIC.

My presentation is __³_____ _____ three sections. __⁴_____ , I will tell you about how the TOEIC is constructed. Secondly, I'm going to __⁵_____ _____ _____ how to prepare for the exam in an efficient way. __⁶_____ , you will pick up some useful problem-solving skills for the TOEIC test.

The presentation will __⁷_____ _____ _____ minutes. And there will be __⁸_____ _____ _____ for refreshments before the Q&A session.

WEEK 05

발표 시작과 전개

Starting and Developing a Presentation

Vocabulary & Expressions

발표 시작하기

- **I will begin by / Let's start with** ~하는 것으로 시작하겠습니다
- **Have you ever wondered ...?** ~을 궁금해한 적이 있습니까?
- **How many people realize that ...?** ~을 몇 분이나 알고 계시나요?
- **Consider for a moment / Think for a moment about** ~에 대해 잠시 생각해보세요

주제 전환하기

- **Let's turn to** ~으로 넘어갑시다
- **Shall we move[go] on to ...?** ~으로 넘어갈까요?
- **Now it's time to discuss** 이제 ~에 대해 논의해볼 시간입니다
- **Let's direct our attention to / Let's pay attention to** ~에 주목해봅시다
- **I want to return to / Let's go back to** ~으로 되돌아가 봅시다

자연스럽게 연결하기

- **So now we come to know that** 따라서 우리는 ~라는 점을 알게 됩니다
- **Now I want to describe** 이제 ~을 설명하고자 합니다
- **And that brings me to** 이제 ~에 이르렀습니다

강조하기

- **We can't emphasize the importance of ... too much.** ~의 중요성을 크게 강조하지 않을 수 없습니다.
- **The main point I want to make is that** 제가 전달하려는 요점은 ~입니다
- **Probably the most important of all is** 아마도 가장 중요한 것은 ~일 겁니다
- **It is no exaggeration to say that** ~라고 해도 전혀 과장이 아닙니다
- **I can speak with confidence that** ~라는 점을 자신 있게 말씀 드릴 수 있습니다
- **I must mention that** ~라는 점은 꼭 말씀 드려야겠군요

Useful Expressions

- Let me start my presentation by quoting Steve Jobs.
  스티브 잡스의 말을 인용하는 것**으로 발표를 시작하겠습니다**.
- Now I want to return to what I was saying.
  이제 제가 말하던 것**으로 돌아가겠습니다.**
- Marketing success is based on content partnerships.
  마케팅의 성공은 콘텐츠 제휴**를 기반으로 합니다.**
- We should prepare for a global depression.
  우리는 세계적인 경기 침체에 **대비해야 합니다.**
- Especially in our case, it is almost imperative.
  특히 우리의 경우엔, 그것이 더욱 필수적입니다.

A Match the meanings on the left with the expressions on the right.

1 차별화하다 •   • ⓐ most innovative

2 가장 혁신적인 •   • ⓑ brief description

3 간략한 설명 •   • ⓒ differentiate

4 장기적인 헌신 •   • ⓓ huge success

5 엄청난 성공 •   • ⓔ long-term commitment

B Fill in the blanks with the given words.

1 시장 조사의 최근 결과로 넘어갑시다.
  ▸ Let's _____ _____ the latest findings of the market research.

2 우리가 직면한 현실에 주목해봅시다.
  ▸ Let's _____ _____ to the reality we're facing, shall we?

3 이제 '퀵 서치'라고 불리는 이 기능을 사용하는 방법을 설명하고자 합니다.
  ▸ Now I want to _____ how to use this feature called "Quick Search".

4 직원의 건강과 안전의 중요성을 크게 강조하지 않을 수가 없습니다.
  ▸ We can't _____ the importance of workers' health and safety _____ _____.

5 현재의 재정 위기에 대한 몇 가지 배경을 말씀 드리는 것으로 시작하겠습니다.
  ▸ I will _____ _____ giving you some background on the current financial crisis.

> **Words**
> pay attention
> turn to
> too much
> begin by
> describe
> emphasize

C Refer to the Korean and fill in the blanks.

1 _____ _____ people realize that the demand for digital camera keeps decreasing?
  디지털 카메라에 대한 수요가 계속 감소하고 있다는 것을 몇 분이나 알고 계시나요?

2 _____ for a moment _____ who your customers are.
  당신의 고객이 누구인지에 대해 잠시만 생각해보세요.

3 Now it's _____ to _____ the competition factors.
  이제 경쟁 요소들에 대해 논의해볼 시간입니다.

4 So now we _____ _____ _____ that this could cause a financial problem.
  그래서 우리는 이것이 재정적인 문제를 초래할 수 있다는 것을 알 수 있게 됩니다.

5 I can speak _____ _____ that such rumors were totally groundless.
  그러한 소문들은 전혀 근거가 없다고 자신 있게 말씀드릴 수 있습니다.

21.mp3

[1]**Let me start my presentation by** sharing with you some of the philosophy behind our overseas operations. The philosophy for our overseas operations is based on a long-term commitment to introduce innovative products. That is the continuous transfer of innovative technology. Especially in the case of a technology company like us, it is almost imperative.

[2]**Let's move on to** the brief history of Sony to back up my argument. Sony was primarily a hardware company. However, in 1995 when Mr. Idei was appointed the COO of Sony, he committed the company to developing service platforms for content distribution. It was a huge success!

Now [3]**I want to return to** what I was going to say. Like Sony, we have to differentiate our business model. How can we then differentiate ourselves from our competition?

Pattern Training

1 **Let me start my presentation by** [_____]. ~으로써 저의 발표를 시작하겠습니다.

① giving you an overview of the French economy
② offering you a brief review of the last 6 months
③ giving you a little background on the mobile phone market

▶ 프랑스 경제에 대한 개요를 설명함 / 지난 6개월 간의 성과를 간략히 보고함 / 휴대전화 시장에 대한 약간의 배경을 설명함

2 **Let's move on to** [_____]. ~으로 넘어갑시다.

① today's agenda
② the next section
③ the issue of workers' compensation

▶ 오늘의 의제 / 다음 부분 / 근로자 보상 문제

🔵 반대 표현

▸ **I'd like to go into detail** about the best way to design a training program.
훈련 프로그램을 설계하는 가장 좋은 방법에 대해 **좀 더 자세히 말씀 드리겠습니다.**

3 **I want to return to** [_____]. ~으로 돌아가겠습니다.

① the third point
② the sales figures of each store
③ the technical features of our music download service

▶ 세 번째 요지 / 각 매장의 매출 수치 / 저희 음악 다운로드 서비스의 기술적 특징

22.mp3

[1]**I can speak with confidence that** a great opportunity lies ahead of us. We should prepare for this new tidal wave when we enter the network age.

Our competitors are totally different today. Now you can see some of the logos and company names such as Samsung and LG. They are both Asian companies.

Let's look at the top five countries with the highest penetration of broadband infrastructure. Four out of those five are Asian countries. [2]**It is no exaggeration to say that** Korea will become one of the most exciting hubs. People here are always willing to adopt new technology. Also, [3]**I must mention that** Korea is a gateway into Asia. I hope you can see the great opportunity to develop new business models in Korea.

Pattern Training

1 **I can speak with confidence that** [_____]. ~라고 자신 있게 말할 수 있습니다.

① this is the best product we've ever made
② we need to restructure our company
③ this plan will have an enormous impact on our future business

▶ 이것이 저희가 만든 제품 중 최고라고 / 우리 회사를 구조조정 해야 한다고 / 이 계획이 우리의 향후 사업에 엄청난 영향을 끼칠 것이라고

2 **It is no exaggeration to say that** [_____]. ~라고 해도 과언이 아닙니다.

① our business is booming
② video games can help create killers
③ this is one of the greatest exhibitions ever held in Canada

▶ 우리 사업이 호황을 누리고 있다고 / 비디오 게임이 살인자를 만들어낼 수 있다고 / 이것이 캐나다에서 열린 최고의 전시회 중 하나라고

3 **I must mention that** [_____]. ~라는 점을 언급해야겠습니다.

① Hong Kong deserves special emphasis
② our planning team is totally unaware of the current market size
③ we are understaffed at the moment

▶ 홍콩이 특별한 주목을 받을 만하다는 / 우리 기획팀이 현재의 시장 규모에 대해 전혀 모르고 있다는 / 현재 우리는 인력이 부족하다는

A Match the phrases with similar meanings.

1 Now I'll focus my discussion on ·   · ⓐ Then we come to the issue of

2 Let's start with ·   · ⓑ Let's go back to

3 Now I want to return to ·   · ⓒ Let's pay attention to

4 That brings me to ·   · ⓓ I will begin by

5 I can speak with confidence that ·   · ⓔ It's no exaggeration to say that

B Choose the best expressions for the blanks and complete the presentations.

ⓐ allow you	ⓑ with confidence	ⓒ no exaggeration
ⓓ let me start	ⓔ move on to	ⓕ must mention
ⓖ in addition to that	ⓗ by introducing	ⓘ take a look

1

_____ my presentation _____ the key features of this cell phone. This cell phone is so light that you can hold it comfortably. I can speak _____ that this is the lightest phone in the world. _____, it uses the latest wireless technology.

Let's _____ its performance. You can continuously talk on the phone for 30 hours, which means its battery lasts longer than others.

이 휴대전화의 주요 특징을 소개함으로써 발표를 시작하겠습니다. 이 휴대전화는 아주 가벼워서 편안하게 잡을 수 있습니다. 세계에서 가장 가벼운 휴대전화라고 자신 있게 말씀드릴 수 있습니다. 그뿐 아니라, 최신 무선 기술을 이용합니다.
성능으로 넘어가죠. 여러분은 연속으로 30시간을 통화할 수 있습니다. 즉, 다른 제품들보다 배터리 수명이 길다는 것이죠.

2

Let's _____ at the major specifications. The keyless entry system will _____ to unlock your car by pushing a button on a remote control.

Do you have kids? The rear-seat entertainment system can make long trips easier for you and them.

It is _____ to say that this car is the most convenient and entertaining car in history. Also, I _____ that its gas mileage is incredible and is a lot better than others.

주요 사양을 살펴봅시다. 열쇠 없는 출입 시스템으로 인해 리모컨의 단추 하나 누름으로써 차 문을 열 수 있습니다.
아이가 있나요? 뒷자리의 엔터테인먼트 시스템은 긴 여행에서 여러분과 아이들이 더 편안하도록 해줄 겁니다.
이 차가 역사상 가장 편리하고 즐거운 차라고 해도 과언이 아닙니다. 또, 연비는 믿을 수 없을 정도이고 다른 차보다 훨씬 뛰어나다는 것을 꼭 말씀 드려야겠군요.

Practice 2　Listen-up!

A　Listen to the presentation and answer the questions.

23.mp3

1 What is the presenter sharing with the audience?

▶ _____

2 What company is the presenter probably working for?

▶ _____

3 What is being shown to the audience?

▶ _____

4 What does the presenter say is a complete failure?

▶ _____

5 How many gas stations does Exxon Shell have?

▶ _____

B　Listen again and complete the blanks.

23.mp3

I would like to start my presentation __1__ _____ _____ our current marketing strategy with you.
Our marketing strategy at the moment __2__ _____ _____ _____ word-of-mouth and oil
quality. However, it hasn't been working fine as you can see from the chart showing our sales
history. Therefore, I __3__ _____ _____ _____ there must be a change in our strategy.

Especially __4__ _____ _____ _____ _____ an oil company like us, gas station locations
are really important. Let's __5__ _____ _____ _____ of Exxon Shell. It has 26,000 gas
stations near almost all of the interstate on- and off-ramps across the nation. It is __6__ _____
_____ _____ _____ that our location strategy is a complete failure.

C　Listen to the presentation and check true or false.

24.mp3

	True	False
1 The presenter wants exact answers to his questions from the audience.		
2 The presenter emphasizes the importance of technology, not design.		
3 The presenter is going to explain how to become a creative designer.		

발표 마무리하기 및 질문받기

Concluding a Presentation and Taking Questions

Vocabulary & Expressions

발표 요약하기

- **Here is a summary of** ~을 요약하면 이렇습니다
- **Let me give you a recap of** ~을 요약하겠습니다
- **Summarizing what we have been discussing,** 지금까지 논의한 것을 요약하면,
- **I'd like to go over ... again.** 다시 ~을 살펴보고자 합니다.
- **To sum up,** 요약하면,
- **To put it briefly,** 간단히 말하면,

발표 끝내기

- **Today we've seen that** 오늘 우리는 ~을 살펴보았습니다
- **In brief, we have looked at** 간략하게, 우리는 ~을 살펴보았습니다.
- **In conclusion, I'd like to emphasize that** 마지막으로, ~라는 것을 강조하고 싶습니다
- **To conclude, I'd like to say that** 끝으로, ~라는 점을 말씀 드리고 싶습니다
- **I'd like to end by** ~하는 것으로 끝마치고자 합니다
- **That concludes** 이것으로 ~을 끝마칩니다
- **Thank you for your attention.** 경청해주셔서 감사합니다

질문받기 및 질문하기

- **Are there any questions? / Do you have any questions?** 질문 있으신가요?
- **I didn't understand what you said about** ~에 대해 말씀하신 내용을 이해 못했습니다
- **Sorry, but I'm not quite clear on** 죄송합니다만, ~에 대해 명확하게 이해가 안 됩니다
- **What did you mean when you said ...?** ~라고 하셨던 게 무슨 의미였죠?
- **I'm not sure what you mean.** 무슨 말씀인지 잘 모르겠네요.

Useful Expressions

- Therefore, it would be easier to handle customer complaints. — 따라서, 고객불만을 다루는 것이 더 쉬워질 것입니다.
- That's a very good question. — **아주 좋은 질문입니다.**
- Thank you very much for your patience and attention. — 인내심을 갖고 경청해주셔서 대단히 감사합니다.
- Sorry, perhaps I did not make that quite clear. — 죄송하지만, **제가 명확하게 말씀 드리지 못한** 것 같습니다.
- If there are no further questions, I think we should stop here. — 더 이상 질문이 없으면 여기서 마치겠습니다.

A Match the meanings on the left with the expressions on the right.

1 끝으로, 마지막으로 ·   · ⓐ market's demands

2 요약하다 ·   · ⓑ for optimization

3 시장의 수요 ·   · ⓒ sum up

4 중요한 요인 ·   · ⓓ crucial factors

5 최적화를 위해 ·   · ⓔ in conclusion

B Fill in the blanks using the given words.

Words
look at
clear on
briefly
put
end by
conclude

1 이것으로 제 발표를 마칩니다.
 ▶ That ＿＿＿＿＿＿ my presentation.

2 간략하게 설문조사 결과를 살펴보았습니다.
 ▶ In brief, we have ＿＿＿＿＿ ＿＿＿＿＿ the results of the questionnaire.

3 죄송합니다만, 제안하시는 내용에 대해 명확하게 이해되지 않는데요.
 ▶ Sorry, but I'm not quite ＿＿＿＿＿ ＿＿＿＿＿ what you're suggesting.

4 간단히 말하면, 이 디자인은 매력적이지 않습니다.
 ▶ To ＿＿＿＿＿ it ＿＿＿＿＿, this design does not look attractive.

5 좀 더 자세하게 연구되어야 할 쟁점들을 지적하면서 끝마칠까 합니다.
 ▶ I'd like to ＿＿＿＿＿ ＿＿＿＿＿ pointing out some issues that need to be studied in more detail.

C Refer to the Korean and fill in the blanks.

1 ＿＿＿＿＿ ＿＿＿＿＿ we have been discussing, the software integration must be done by August 8.
우리가 논의한 것을 요약하자면, 소프트웨어 통합은 8월 8일까지 마무리되어야 합니다.

2 I didn't understand ＿＿＿＿＿ ＿＿＿＿＿ ＿＿＿＿＿ about the new firmware.
새로운 펌웨어에 대해 말씀한 내용을 이해 못했습니다.

3 In ＿＿＿＿＿, I'd like to ＿＿＿＿＿ that we're going through a very crucial juncture of this era.
마지막으로, 우리는 현재 이 시대의 가장 중요한 시기를 겪고 있다는 것을 강조하고 싶습니다.

4 ＿＿＿＿＿ you so much ＿＿＿＿＿ your patience and attention.
끝까지 인내해주시고 경청해주셔서 대단히 감사합니다.

5 Do you have any ＿＿＿＿＿ on these rights?
이러한 권리에 대해서 질문 있으세요?

25.mp3

[1]**Let me sum up** what I've just said so far.

First, we have made our cost structures more flexible. Therefore, we are in a much better position to respond to the market's demands. Second, we have already achieved significant improvements in operational efficiency. Third, we are constantly working to leverage our potential for optimization. These are evidence of the strength our company has built up over the past few years.

[2]**In conclusion**, we will be working to ensure they continue. Thank you very much indeed for your patience and attention. [3]**I especially appreciate** your struggle to keep awake during this extremely sleepy time of the day.

Pattern Training

1   **Let me sum up** [_____]. ~을 요약하겠습니다.

① the main points again
② what happened this year
③ what we have decided

▶ 다시 한 번 주요 부분 / 올해 있었던 일 / 우리가 결정한 것

2   **In conclusion,** [_____]. 마지막으로, ~. / 결론적으로, ~.

① please keep in mind that we are here to win
② we hope that our suggestions prove to be useful
③ we found that the chocolate chips have the most fat

▶ 우리가 성취하기 위해 이 자리에 있다는 것을 명심해주세요 / 저희 제안이 도움이 되기를 바랍니다 / 초콜릿 칩이 가장 많은 지방을 함유하고 있다는 것을 알아냈습니다

3   **I especially appreciate** [_____]. ~에 특히 감사를 표합니다.

① your input
② you for what you've done
③ that you took your time to attend this conference

▶ 귀하가 제공해주신 정보에 / 해주신 일에 대해 여러분께 / 회의 참석을 위해 시간을 내주신 것에

26.mp3

A   [1]**That concludes** my presentation. [2]**Are there any questions on** what I've told you so far?

B   Dr. Royal, this is Christine. So what do you think the most crucial factors are in setting up a successful business?

A   Well, that's a very good question. I think one of the key things in Europe is to be ambitious. However, most importantly, we've got to be realistic.

B   [3]**I don't see** what you mean.

A   Sorry, perhaps I did not make that quite clear. Let's say you want to be the number-one book seller in the UK. However, in order to achieve your ambition, you have to realistically analyze the risk factors associated with the UK market.

B   I totally agree with you.

A   Thank you. Are there any more questions? If there are no further questions, I think we should stop here.

Pattern Training

1   **That concludes** ⌐‾‾‾‾‾‾‾‾‾‾‾¬. 이것으로 ~을 마칩니다.

① what I have to say tonight
② my two-hour presentation
③ our video presentation on this topic

▶ 오늘 저녁에 전해드릴 말 / 두 시간에 걸친 제 발표 / 이 주제에 관한 비디오 발표

2   **Are there any questions on** ⌐‾‾‾‾‾‾‾‾‾‾¬? ~에 대해 질문 있으십니까?

① any of my comments
② the following topics
③ anything we've discussed

▶ 제 논평 / 다음 주제들 / 우리가 논의한 것들

3   **I don't see** ⌐‾‾‾‾‾‾‾‾‾‾¬. ~을 알 수가 없네요.

① what you're referring to
② what you're talking about
③ what you're getting at

▶ 무엇을 언급하시는지 / 무슨 말씀을 하시는 건지 / 무엇을 말씀하시려고 하는 건지

A Make sentences using the given words.

further questions / stop	conclude / demonstration	questions / what I've told you
thank / attention	sum up / discuss	see / mean

1 이것으로 우리의 새로운 소프트웨어에 대한 시연회를 마칩니다.

▶ _____

2 경청해주셔서 대단히 감사합니다.

▶ _____

3 무슨 말씀인지 모르겠습니다.

▶ _____

4 지금까지 논의한 내용을 요약하겠습니다.

▶ Let _____

5 제가 지금까지 말씀 드린 것에 관해 질문 있으신가요?

▶ Are _____

6 더 이상 질문 없으시면 여기서 마치고자 합니다.

▶ _____

B Choose the best expressions for the blanks and complete the dialogs.

ⓐ that covers all	ⓑ as I've told you so far	ⓒ thank you for
ⓓ it's time	ⓔ wrap it up	ⓕ it depends on

1

_____ to end my presentation. _____, we have to reform our company structure immediately. That's the only way to remain competitive in this market.

_____ listening.

발표를 마칠 시간이군요. 지금까지 말씀 드렸듯이, 회사 구조를 즉시 개선해야 합니다. 그것이 이 시장에서 경쟁력을 유지하는 유일한 방법입니다.
경청해주셔서 감사합니다.

2

A: _____ that I wanted to say tonight. Are there any questions?

B: You said that we should boost worker morale. But you didn't mention how.

A: Well, _____ what kind of working environment they are in. You should come up with how to make them happy. Any more questions? If there are no other questions, why don't we _____ here?

A: 이것으로 오늘 저녁 제가 하고자 했던 얘기는 모두 끝났습니다. 질문 있습니까?
B: 직원의 사기를 올려야 한다고 말씀하셨습니다. 그러나 방법은 말씀해주지 않으셨네요.
A: 음, 그건 직원들이 어떤 업무 환경에 처해 있느냐에 따라 다릅니다. 여러분께서 어떻게 하면 직원들을 만족시킬 수 있을지를 연구하셔야 합니다. 질문 더 있으신가요? 다른 질문이 없으면 여기서 끝마칠까요?

A   Listen to the presentation and check true or false.

27.mp3

	True	False
1 The speaker is in the instant food business.		
2 VegeTwo has superior technology in the latest product generation.		
3 VegeTwo has been in business for 50 years.		
4 VegeTwo is somewhat slow to adapt to market needs.		

B   Listen again and complete the blanks.

27.mp3

Now ¹_____ _____ _____ _____ my presentation with an outlook for our business. ²_____ , we are one of the global leaders in the health food business. ³_____ , we have a very strong asset base with superior technology in the latest product generation. ⁴_____ _____ _____ _____ that we, VegeTwo, are one of the innovation drivers. ⁵_____ , 50 years of tradition and industrial knowledge ⁶_____ _____ _____ _____ enables us to quickly respond to market requirements.

⁷_____ _____ , we always keep track of the global market mega trends ⁸_____ _____ _____ ensure long-term success. Thank you.

C   Listen to the presentation and complete the sentences.

28.mp3

1 The presenter gave a speech about ┊_____┊ before the Q&A session.

2 It was announced at ┊_____┊ in Stockholm that this biotechnology is very stable.

3 The new product equipped with the technology will be shown in ┊_____┊

시각자료 사용 및 효과적인 분석

Visual Aids and Effective Analysis

Vocabulary & Expressions

시각자료 소개 및 설명하기

- **I'd like to show you ... / I have ... to show you.** 여러분께 ~을 보여드리겠습니다
- **Let's take a look at** ~을 봅시다
- **I'd like us to pay attention to / I'd like us to concentrate on** ~에 집중해주시기 바랍니다
- **This represents** 이것은 ~을 나타냅니다 (represent = show, indicate, stand for)
- **Looking at ~, you will see that ...** ~을 보면 …을 알 수 있을 겁니다
- **As you can see from ~, ...** ~에서 알 수 있듯이 …입니다

자료 분석하기

- **increase / rise / go up / improve** 증가하다 • **shoot up / soar** 치솟다
- **decrease / fall / decline / go down** 감소하다
- **slump** 급락하다 • **slow down** 둔화되다
- **reach a peak** 최고치에 도달하다 • **hit bottom** 최저치에 도달하다
- **stabilize** 안정되다 • **fluctuate** 오르락내리락하다
- **account for** (비율을) 차지하다

대조 및 비교하기

- **on the other hand** 반면에
- **while** ~하는 반면
- **in contrast to** ~와는 대조적으로
- **in comparison with[to]** ~와 비교해서
- **A differs from B** A는 B와 다르다

증거 및 근거 제시하기

- **Experts estimate that** 전문가들은 ~라고 추정한다
- **Statistics show that** 통계에 따르면 ~이다
- **Based on** ~에 근거하면
- **According to** ~에 따르면
- **for example** 예를 들면

Plus Vocabulary

- **bar graph** 막대 그래프
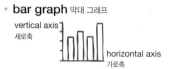
vertical axis 세로축 / horizontal axis 가로축

- **line graph** 선 그래프

solid line 실선 / dotted line 점선

- **pie chart** 원형 차트
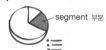
segment 부분

- **table** 도표

row 행 / cell 칸 / column 열

Useful Expressions

- Let's take a look at this line graph.

  이 선 그래프를 봅시다.

- Could you please dim the lights a bit?

  불빛을 좀 흐리게 해주시겠어요?

- As you can see from the chart, we spent $5,000 on R&D.

  차트에서 알 수 있듯이, 우리는 연구개발에 5,000달러를 썼습니다.

- On the other hand, investments in marketing dropped.

  반면, 마케팅 투자액은 떨어졌습니다.

- As a direct result, we have experienced a lot of success.

  직접적인 결과로서, 우리는 큰 성공을 거두었습니다.

Vocabulary Check-Up

A Match the meanings on the left with the expressions on the right.

1	장비, 비품 ·	· ⓐ	handout
2	유인물, 인쇄물 ·	· ⓑ	statistics
3	애쓰다, 고심하다 ·	· ⓒ	equipment
4	통계자료 ·	· ⓓ	concentrate on
5	~에 집중하다 ·	· ⓔ	struggle

B Fill in the blanks using the given words.

1 우리의 6월 판매량은 10% 증가했습니다.
▶ Our June sales ＿＿＿＿＿ ＿＿＿＿＿ 10%.

2 점선은 예상 성장률을 나타냅니다.
▶ The dotted line ＿＿＿＿＿ the projected growth.

3 이 실선에 집중해주시기 바랍니다.
▶ I'd like us to ＿＿＿＿＿ ＿＿＿＿＿ this solid line.

4 홍콩의 산업 성장이 11월에 둔화되었습니다.
▶ Hong Kong's industrial growth ＿＿＿＿＿ ＿＿＿＿＿ in November.

5 도표를 보시면 주요 휴대전화 재판매업자들을 볼 수 있을 겁니다.
▶ If you ＿＿＿＿ ＿＿＿＿ ＿＿＿＿ at the table, you will ＿＿＿＿ the major resellers of mobile phones.

> **Words**
> represent
> concentrate on
> take a look
> see
> increase by
> slow down

C Refer to the Korean and fill in the blanks.

1 The ＿＿＿＿ ＿＿＿＿ shows the day of the month and the ＿＿＿＿ ＿＿＿＿ shows the local time.
가로축은 날짜를 나타내고 세로축은 현지 시간을 나타냅니다.

2 In the ＿＿＿＿, we have listed our current vendors.
행에는 현재 우리가 거래하는 업체들을 나열했습니다.

3 ＿＿＿＿ ＿＿＿＿ to previous years, there has been a decline in share ownership.
예년과 비교해서, 주식 소유 지분에 감소가 있었습니다.

4 ＿＿＿＿ a direct ＿＿＿＿, we lost a lot of money.
직접적인 결과로서, 우리는 엄청난 돈을 잃었습니다.

5 Their market share ＿＿＿＿ ＿＿＿＿ 8%, which is up 4% from last year's figure.
그들의 시장점유율이 8%로 치솟았습니다. 이것은 작년 수치에서 4% 상승한 것입니다.

29.mp3

¹**I have** some charts **to show you**.

²**If you take a look at** this bar graph, **you will see that** last year we spent more money on R&D than on marketing. ³**As you can see from** the chart on the screen, we spent $1,000 on R&D, which is an increase of 30% in comparison to the year before last year. On the other hand, the investment in marketing dropped by 30%.

However, now it's time to focus more on marketing to let people know about our products. Let's have a look at this line graph. It shows our rivals' spending on marketing. They spent nearly twice as much money on marketing as we did last year.

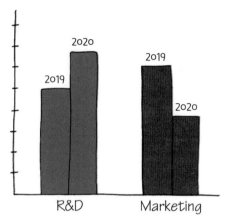

Pattern Training

1 **I have** [＿＿＿＿＿] **to show you.** 여러분께 보여드릴 ~이 있습니다.

① something
② some graphs
③ some products

▶ 어떤 것 / 그래프 몇 개 / 제품 몇 개

2 **If you take a look at** [＿＿＿＿＿], **you will see that** [＿＿＿＿＿].
…을 보면, ~라는 것을 알 수 있을 겁니다.

① this table, our ad revenue softened
② this flow chart, the Chinese oil demand has been picking up
③ this pie chart, there seems to be a downward trend in the consumer price index

▶ 이 도표, 우리의 광고 수입이 낮아졌다 / 이 순서도, 중국의 석유 수요가 오르고 있다 / 이 원형 차트, 소비자 물가지수에 하강 추세가 있어 보인다

3 **As you can see from** [＿＿＿＿＿], [＿＿＿＿＿]. …에서 알 수 있듯이, ~.

① the pictures, the key to success is to understand the market trends
② the feedback below, this year's performance has been a great success
③ the statistics, there are many factors besides tires that affect the amount of fuel

▶ 그림들, 성공의 비결은 시장의 동향을 이해하는 것입니다 / 아래의 피드백, 올해의 성과는 아주 좋았습니다 / 통계, 타이어 외에도 연료량에 영향을 주는 많은 요소가 있습니다

30.mp3

Our sales are holding steady even though we are new to the Japanese market. [1]**On the other hand**, many of our competitors are struggling to boost their sales. According to the report from the Sales Department, we sold 1,500 vehicles in the last year alone.

By the way, could you please take a look at the handout that I distributed? As you can see from the chart on it, our sales in China were down 30% compared to a year ago. [2]**In contrast to** the Japanese market, our sales in China have slowed down.

But we don't have to worry about the slow sales there. As you might know, we are planning to open a marketing office in China late this year. [3]**As a direct result**, we are expecting to be able to generate profits in the Chinese market as well.

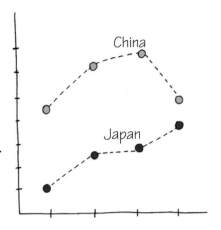

Pattern Training

1   **On the other hand,** ☐. 반면에, ~.

① I'm convinced that we will enjoy strong sales growth next year
② we did not lose any money in the domestic market
③ the overall employee satisfaction level is high

▶ 내년에는 높은 매출 성장세를 누릴 것으로 확신합니다 / 국내 시장에서 손해를 보지는 않았습니다 / 전반적인 직원 만족도가 높습니다

2   **In contrast to** ☐ **,** ☐. …와는 대조적으로, ~.

① their expectation, this system will save us a lot of money
② last year, economic growth this year is expected to increase by 4%
③ the report, large teams can achieve high levels of cooperation

▶ 그들의 예상, 이 시스템은 많은 돈을 절약할 수 있게 해줄 것입니다 / 작년, 올해의 경제 성장률은 4% 오를 것으로 예상됩니다 / 그 보고서, 규모가 큰 팀이 높은 수준의 협동성을 이룩할 수 있습니다

3   **As a direct result,** ☐. 그 직접적인 결과로서, ~.

① working hours have been prolonged
② we finally won the contract with the company from England
③ the company has recognized Janet as the employee of the year

▶ 근무시간이 늘었습니다 / 마침내 영국 회사와의 계약을 땄습니다 / 회사에서 올해의 직원으로 자넷을 인정했습니다

A Make sentences using the given words.

1 화면에 나와 있는 차트를 봐주세요. (take a look)

▶ _____

2 이 수치는 고객센터에서 올라온 보고서에 근거한 것입니다. (be based on / customer service center)

▶ _____

3 판매량이 감소한 반면, 불량품은 늘었습니다. (while / increase / drop)

▶ _____

4 한 설문조사에 따르면, 사람들은 영화를 일주일에 두 번 보고 있습니다. (according to / twice a week)

▶ _____

5 쌀 소비량을 나타내는 점선에 주목해주세요. (I'd like us to / pay attention to / represent)

▶ _____

B Choose the best expressions for the blanks.

ⓐ represents	ⓑ shows the percentages	ⓒ while	ⓓ we can see
ⓔ take a look	ⓕ as you can see	ⓖ accounts for	ⓗ the biggest segment

1

Now _____ at the line graph.

It shows the sales of gold in LA for 6 months in 2019. The vertical axis _____ the amount of money in dollars _____ the horizontal axis represents the months of the year from January through June.

Clearly, _____ that our sales have sharply increased.

이제 선 그래프를 보시죠.
이 그래프는 2019년 6개월 동안 LA에서의 금 판매량을 보여주고 있습니다. 가로축은 1월부터 6월까지의 달을 나타내는 한편, 세로축은 금액을 달러로 나타내고 있습니다.
명확하게, 우리의 매출이 현저히 증가했다는 것을 알 수 있습니다.

2

This pie chart _____ of people who follow various religions in the United States.

Let's begin with _____, which is Christianity, in red. We can see that 55% of the total population is Christian. _____ from the blue segment here, Buddhism only _____ 5% of the population in the United States.

이 원형 차트는 미국에서 다양한 종교를 믿는 사람들의 비율을 나타내고 있습니다.
가장 큰 부분인 빨간색으로 된 기독교부터 시작하겠습니다. 우리는 전체 인구의 55%가 기독교인이라는 것을 알 수 있습니다. 여기 파란색 부분에서 알 수 있듯이, 불교는 미국 내 인구의 겨우 5%를 차지하고 있습니다.

A   Listen to the presentation and complete the blanks.   31.mp3

million

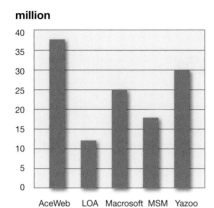

billion

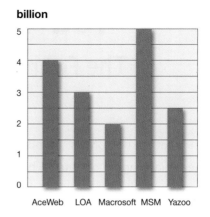

1   The audience gap between first and last place is about [＿＿＿＿] million people.

2   In terms of page views, the difference between MSM and Macrosoft is roughly [＿＿＿＿] billion page views.

B   Listen to the presentation and check true or false.   32.mp3

	True	False
1 The topic of the presentation is the viewership of news programs.		
2 Radio news listener ratings declined because of the increasing use of personal radios.		
3 People who listen to the news on the radio can use their computers at the same time.		

C   Listen again and complete the blanks.   32.mp3

Our television news programs are in trouble with the American public. _¹＿＿＿＿＿ ＿＿＿＿

＿＿＿＿ ＿＿＿＿, the viewership of our nightly news has been particularly hard hit. _²＿＿＿＿

＿＿＿＿, the percentage of people who listen to radio news programs is largely the same as it

has been over the past three years.

_³＿＿＿ ＿＿＿＿ ＿＿＿＿ the decline in TV news viewing _⁴＿＿＿ ＿＿＿＿ ＿＿＿＿

＿＿＿＿ the increasing use of smartphones. However, listening to radio news, which usually

occurs while doing some other tasks, _⁵＿＿＿ ＿＿＿＿ ＿＿＿＿ among smartphone users.

Ted Turner
"The Founder of CNN"

On September 18, 1997, Ted Turner, CNN's [1]**founder** and Time Warner's vice chairman, announced Friday evening that he is planning to [2]**donate** $1 billion to United Nations programs.

Turner made the announcement at a dinner held in Los Angeles by the United Nations Association. The purpose of the dinner was to honor Turner for his [3]**remarkable contribution** to the international community. He was also [4]**awarded** the Global Leadership award by the representative of the group.

[5]**Speaking of** his gift, Turner said, "This is not going to go for administration. This is only going to go for programs, like cleaning up land mines, peacekeeping, refugees, UNICEF for the children, and the money can only go to U.N. causes."

Turner now [6]**dedicates** his time and money to making the world a better and safer place to live for future generations. In addition, he remains energetically involved in business with the rapidly expanding Montana Grill restaurant chain.

© Louis.Roth/shutterstock

© EQRoy/shutterstock

1997년 9월 18일, CNN 창립자이자 타임워너 부회장인 테드 터너는 금요일 저녁 UN 프로그램에 십억 달러를 기부할 것이라고 발표했다.

UN연합이 LA에서 개최한 저녁 만찬에서 그는 이와 같이 발표했다. 저녁 만찬의 목적은 국제사회에 대한 터너의 괄목할 만한 공헌을 기리고자 하는 것이었다. 그는 또한 그룹 대표로부터 글로벌 리더십 상을 받았다.

그의 기부에 대해 터너는 "이 기부금은 UN행정부를 위해 쓰일 것이 아니다. 지뢰 제거 활동, 평화 유지 활동, 피난민들, 유니세프 아동 기금 등과 같은 프로그램을 위해서만 사용될 것이다. 그리고 돈은 오로지 UN의 명분에 맞게만 쓰일 것이다."라고 말했다.

터너는 현재 미래 세대가 살기에 더 좋고 안전한 세상을 만들기 위해 자신의 시간과 돈을 바치고 있다.

1 **founder** 창립자, 창시자

Who is the **founder** of the Microsoft?

마이크로소프트의 창립자는 누구인가?

2 **donate** ~을 기부하다

I decided to **donate** the car because selling it seemed like a hassle.

그 차를 파는 것이 복잡해 보여서 나는 그 차를 기부하기로 결정했다.

3 **remarkable contribution** 혁혁한 공헌

He made a **remarkable contribution** to the company's success.

그는 회사의 성공에 엄청난 공을 세웠다.

4 **award** 상을 수여하다

Richard Freedman was **awarded** the Nobel Peace Prize.

리처드 프리드먼이 노벨 평화상을 받았다.

5 **speaking of** ~에 대해 말하자면

Speaking of my boss, she's fair, funny, supportive, smart, and reasonable.

내 상사에 대해 말하자면, 그녀는 공정하고 재미있고 협조적이고 영리하고 합리적이다.

6 **dedicate** 헌납하다, (생애·시간 등을) 바치다

I'd like to **dedicate** my book to my father.

나는 이 책을 아버지께 바치고 싶다.

© Kunal Mehta/shutterstock

Who is Ted Turner?

1938년 11월 19일 생. 미국 굴지의 24시간 유선방송 CNN의 창립자이자 위대한 사회사업가이다. 그의 사업가 마인드는 그가 24세 때 아버지가 자살한 후 물려받은 간판 사업에서 시작되었다. 1980년에 세계 최초로 24시간 동안 뉴스를 방영하는 채널 CNN을 설립하여, 누구나 원하는 시간에 뉴스를 항상 볼 수 있는 새로운 시대를 열었다. 그 후에도 각종 미디어 사업을 키워나가며 큰 성공을 거두었다. 또한 그는 사업가로서뿐만 아니라 UN에 십억 달러를 기부함으로써 사회사업가로도 명성을 날리게 되었다.

© Albert H. Teich/shutterstock

Ted Turner says...

"As I started getting rich, I started thinking, 'What the hell am I going to do with all this money?'... You have to learn to give."

부자가 되면서 '나는 도대체 이 많은 돈으로 무얼 해야 하지?'라고 생각하기 시작했다. 당신은 주는 법을 배워야 한다.

"War has been good to me from a financial standpoint, but I don't want to make money that way. I don't want blood money."

전쟁은 돈벌이 입장에서 보면 나에게 좋은 일이다. 하지만 그런 식으로 돈을 벌고 싶지 않다. 피 묻은 돈은 싫다.

"My son is now an entrepreneur. That's what you're called when you don't have a job."

내 아들은 이제 사업가다. 그게 바로 직업이 없을 때 사람들이 부르는 말이지.

Practical Business
Performing Tasks Efficiently

PART 3
효율적인 업무 진행

업무 지시하기 및 협조 요청하기

Directing Tasks and Asking for Help

Vocabulary & Expressions

지시하기

- **I'd like you to / I want you to** 당신이 ~해줬으면 좋겠어요
- **Can you take over ...?** ~을 맡아줄래요?
- **Be sure to** 반드시 ~해주세요
- **Please** ~하세요

부탁하기

- **Can you do me a favor? / Could I ask you a favor?**
  부탁 하나 들어줄 수 있어요?
- **Would you give me a hand?** 좀 도와줄 수 있나요?
- **Would[Could] you please ... for me?** 저를 위해서 ~해줄 수 있을까요?
- **Do you have a few minutes to help me with ...?**
  ~하는 데 도와줄 시간 좀 있어요?
- **Can you help me ...?** ~하는 걸 도와줄 수 있어요?
- **I'm sorry to trouble you, but** 폐를 끼쳐서 죄송하지만 (trouble = bother)

도움 제안하기

- **Shall I ...?** 제가 ~할까요?
- **Would you like me to ...?** 제가 ~ 해드릴까요?
- **I will give you a hand.** 제가 도와드릴게요.
- **I can help you with** ~을 도와드릴 수 있어요

💿 Plus Expression

부탁을 받아들이는 대답

- **Okay.** 알겠습니다.
- **I'd be glad to.** 기꺼이 그러죠.
- **Yes, sure.** 네, 그러죠.
- **No problem.** 그럼요.

부탁을 거절하는 대답

- **I'd rather not.** 안 되겠는데요.
- **I'm rather busy.** 좀 바쁜데요.
- **I'm sorry, but I can't do it.** 죄송하지만 못하겠어요.
- **It's a difficult task.** 무리한 요구인데요.

Useful Expressions

- I'd like you to install the network system.   당신이 네트워크 시스템을 설치해주었으면 합니다.

- I can't make it to the workshop.   워크숍에 갈 수가 없어요.

- You're going to owe me big time.   당신 나한테 큰 신세 진 거예요.

- Let's get back to work!   자, 일들 합시다!

- I've got my hands full at the moment.   지금은 아주 바빠요.

Vocabulary Check-Up

A Match the meanings on the left with the expressions on the right.

1 호의 •

2 이달 말 •

3 하루 종일 •

4 고객만족도 조사 •

5 ~에게 크게 신세 지다 •

• ⓐ customer satisfaction survey

• ⓑ favor

• ⓒ owe *someone* big time

• ⓓ the end of this month

• ⓔ all day long

B Fill in the blanks with the given words.

1 그 요약본을 당신이 전 직원에게 이메일로 보냈으면 합니다.
  ▸ I'd _____ _____ to email the summary to the entire staff.

2 이 파일 좀 열어주실래요?
  ▸ _____ _____ please open this file for me?

3 도움이 필요하면 저한테 말하세요.
  ▸ If you need _____ _____, just let me know.

4 퇴근하기 전에 초안을 확실히 끝내놓으세요.
  ▸ _____ _____ to finish the preliminary draft before you leave.

5 폐를 끼쳐서 죄송하지만 이 계약서를 좀 검토해주실래요?
  ▸ I'm sorry to _____ _____, but could you go over this contract?

> Words
> any help
> be sure
> trouble you
> would you
> like you

C Refer to the Korean and fill in the blanks.

1 Who can _____ me a _____ and solve my coding problems?
  누가 이 코딩 문제 해결하는 걸 도와줄 수 있죠?

2 Can you help me _____ the finance data?
  지금 데이터 분석하는 걸 도와줄 수 있어요?

3 Could I ask you _____ _____?
  부탁 하나 해도 될까요?

4 Can you _____ _____ the management of our website?
  우리 웹사이트 관리를 당신이 맡아줄 수 있어요?

5 Do you _____ a few _____ to help me with the data migration tool?
  이 데이터 마이그레이션 툴 다루는 것 좀 도와줄 시간 돼요?

A There are several tasks to be done by the end of this month.
As you all know, we're going to conduct a customer satisfaction survey on our new product.
Kelly, **¹can I leave it to you**?

B All right. I'll do that.

A Jack, please create a February sales report.

C No problem.

A Norah, **²I'd like you to** attend the meeting with our clients this afternoon.

D Sorry, Mr. Ferraro. I'm fully booked for the day.
So **³I'm afraid that I can't** make it to the meeting.

A I see. Then I will attend the meeting instead.
Okay, that is it. Let's get back to work!

Pattern Training

1 **Can I leave it to you** [＿＿＿＿]**?** 당신에게 ~을 맡겨도 될까요?

① to figure out how to operate the system
② to prepare the presentation
③ to reserve a table at the restaurant

▶ 그 시스템 작동법을 숙지하는 것 / 발표 준비하는 것 / 식당에 자리 예약하는 것

2 **I'd like you to** [＿＿＿＿]**.** 당신이 ~해줬으면 합니다.

① review the report
② check our inventory status
③ arrange a meeting with them

▶ 보고서를 검토해 / 재고 상태를 점검해 / 그들과 회의를 잡아

3 **I'm afraid that I can't** [＿＿＿＿]**.** 아무래도 ~할 수 없겠습니다.

① help you with the presentation
② finish the customer survey by next week
③ host the workshop

▶ 발표를 도울 / 다음 주까지 고객 여론조사를 끝낼 / 워크숍을 주최할

Asking for a favor 도움 요청하기

34.mp3

A Paul, are you busy? Can you do me a favor?

B What's that?

A I have a meeting this afternoon. **¹Can you** finish the rest of the marketing report **for me**? I've got something else to handle immediately.

B I've actually got my hands full at the moment.

A I need your help, Paul.

B Well, **²you can't expect me to** work on it all day long, **can you?**

A No, **³it shouldn't take that much time to** finish it.

B Hmm… Then I may be able to, but you're going to owe me big time.

Pattern Training

1   **Can you** [_____] **for me?** 저 대신 ~해줄 수 있어요?

① book a flight
② make a hotel reservation
③ deal with the customer complaints
▶ 비행기 예약해 / 호텔 예약해 / 고객 불만을 처리해

2   **You can't expect me to** [_____]**, can you?** 설마 제가 ~하기를 기대하는 건 아니죠?

① be a perfect person
② finish it within one day
③ be there during working hours
▶ 완벽한 사람이기를 / 하루 만에 그것을 끝내기를 / 업무 시간에 거기 있기를

3   **It shouldn't take that much time to** [_____].
~하는 데 그리 많은 시간이 걸리진 않아요.

① fix the problem
② draft the report
③ get things under control again
▶ 그 문제를 해결하는 / 보고서의 초안을 잡는 / 다시 상황을 수습하는

A Complete the short dialogs with the given words.

give	full	take	favor
urgent	please	hand	like

1 A: Could you ＿＿＿＿＿＿ over the running of this project?

  B: Sorry, but I'm tied up with something ＿＿＿＿＿＿ these days.

  이 프로젝트의 운영을 맡아주실래요? – 죄송합니다만, 요즘 급한 일로 매우 바빠요.

2 A: Can you do me a ＿＿＿＿＿＿?

  B: I've got my hands ＿＿＿＿＿＿ this week getting ready to leave the company.

  부탁 하나 들어줄래요? – 이번 주에는 퇴사 준비를 하느라 무척 바빠요.

3 A: Would you ＿＿＿＿＿＿ me a ＿＿＿＿＿＿ with this report?

  B: Sure. What's wrong with it?

  이 보고서 좀 도와줄래요? – 그러죠. 뭐가 문제예요?

4 A: Would you ＿＿＿＿＿＿ me to edit chapter 2 of the report?

  B: Yes, ＿＿＿＿＿＿. Hamilton edited it yesterday, but it's full of mistakes.

  보고서 2장을 제가 좀 수정해드릴까요? – 네, 부탁해요. 해밀턴이 어제 수정했는데 실수투성이에요.

B Put the Korean into English and complete the dialogs.

1

A: 전시회 준비는 어떻게 되어가고 있어요? (how / go)

B: Several products to be displayed aren't working fine.

A: 그 제품들에 무슨 문제가 있는데요? (wrong)

B: We don't know yet.

A: The IFA show is only 2 weeks from today.

  당신이 가능한 한 빨리 수리를 했으면 합니다. (I'd like you to / repair)

  Please hurry up!

2

A: What's wrong with you?

B: I have an important presentation with the boss tonight.

  하지만 이 프로젝터를 제대로 작동시킬 수가 없어요. (get ... to work / projector)

  It doesn't project anything when I turn it on.

A: That's weird. Maybe the light bulb needs to be replaced.

  그것을 점검할 수리기사를 불러줄까요? (Can I ...? / technician / take a look)

  You seem to be in a hurry preparing for the presentation right now.

B: Thank you so much!

Practice 2 — Listen-up!

A

Listen to the dialog and answer the questions.　　　　　35.mp3

1 Why does Jade look depressed?

ⓐ Her client wants to get a refund.

ⓑ Her client wants to open the website earlier than planned.

ⓒ Her client wants to help David.

ⓓ Her client wants to cancel the website project.

2 What will David's responsibility probably be?

ⓐ He will be responsible for testing the beta version of the website.

ⓑ He will be responsible for scheduling the project.

ⓒ He will be responsible for handling customers' complaints.

ⓓ He will be responsible for helping Jade with the marketing report.

B

Listen again and complete the blanks.　　　　　35.mp3

David: You __1_____ _____. What's up, Jade?

Jade: I just spoke with my client over the phone. He wants to __2_____ _____ _____ _____ of the website to June 6. So, I should __3_____ _____ _____ after work this week.

David: That's too bad. Would you like me __4_____ _____ _____ _____ _____ ?

Jade: Really? __5_____ _____ _____ _____ _____ _____, David.

David: What do you want me to do first?

Jade: __6_____ _____ _____ _____ _____ _____ to test the beta version of the website?

David: No problem.

Jade: Thanks, David.

David: That's what colleagues are for.

C

Listen to the monolog and check true or false.　　　　　36.mp3

	True	False
1 They have a workshop early next week.		
2 Andy has to modify some steps in the workshop procedure.		
3 Maria is responsible for making a list of the items needed.		
4 Jeff is responsible for checking the number of attendees.		

VOCABULARY　CONVERSATION　**PRACTICE**　73

업무 진행 상황 체크하기

Checking the Status of Tasks

Vocabulary & Expressions

진행상황 점검하기

- **I'm wondering if you're done with** ~을 끝냈는지 궁금하네요
- **Could you let me know the status of ...?**
  ~의 상황을 알려주실래요?
- **Please tell me how ... is going so far.**
  ~이 지금까지 어떻게 진행되고 있는지 알려주세요.
- **How far along are you with ...?** ~은 얼마나 진척되었어요?
- **When can you give me ... by?** ~을 내게 언제까지 줄 수 있어요?
- **When are you going to finish ...?** ~을 언제 끝낼 건가요?

진행상황 보고하기

- **... is going according to schedule.**
  ~이 일정대로 진행되고 있어요.
- **It is ... behind schedule.** ~만큼 늦어지고 있어요.
- **It is ... ahead of schedule.** ~만큼 앞서가고 있어요.
- **I'm almost done with** ~을 거의 끝냈습니다
- **It may be slightly later than** ~보다 조금 늦어질 수 있습니다

업무 일정 조율하기

- **Can we bring forward ...?**
  ~의 일정을 앞당길 수 있을까요?
- **I'd like to put ... back.**
  ~의 일정을 뒤로 미뤘으면 합니다.
- **When do you think ... will be done[finished/completed]?**
  ~이 언제 끝날 것으로 생각하세요?
- **It should be finished by / It has to be done before**
  ~까지 마무리되어야 합니다

업무 일정 독촉하기

- **You'd better finish ~ by ...**
  ~을 …까지 끝내는 것이 좋을 겁니다
- **You should ... as fast as you can.**
  할 수 있는 한 빨리 ~해야 합니다.
- **We have to hurry to finish ... on time.**
  ~을 제때에 끝내려면 서둘러야 합니다.
- **We are running out of time.** 시간이 없어요.
- **This is the final warning.** 이것이 마지막 경고입니다.

Useful Expressions

- Can you give me three more days?
- I've been busy finalizing the contract.
- I'll do my best to fend off our competitors.
- Employees' safety is our main priority.
- It's almost done.

3일만 더 주시겠어요?

계약서를 마무리하느라고 바빴습니다.

경쟁사들을 물리치기 위해 최선을 다하겠습니다.

직원들의 안전이 최우선입니다.

거의 끝나갑니다.

Vocabulary Check-Up

A Match the meanings on the left with the expressions on the right.

1 최선을 다하다　　　　　　·　　　　　　· ⓐ work out

2 하반기　　　　　　　　　·　　　　　　· ⓑ do one's best

3 매출 실적　　　　　　　·　　　　　　· ⓒ the second half of the year

4 (문제를) 풀다, 해결하다 ·　　　　　　· ⓓ a final copy

5 최종 사본　　　　　　　·　　　　　　· ⓔ sales performance

B Fill in the blanks using the given words.

Words
one's best
ahead of
better finish
bring forward
slightly later

1 워크숍을 하루 앞당길 수 있을까요?
  ▶ Can we _____ _____ the workshop by a day?

2 정오까지는 사진 업로드를 끝내놓는 게 좋겠습니다.
  ▶ You'd _____ _____ uploading the photos by noon.

3 그 프로젝트는 일정보다 일주일 빠릅니다.
  ▶ The project is one week _____ _____ schedule.

4 납기일이 임시 스케줄에 나와 있는 것보다 조금 더 늦을 수도 있습니다.
  ▶ The deadline may be _____ _____ than what is listed on the tentative schedule.

5 이 웹사이트가 고객들에게 귀중한 자산이 되도록 하기 위해 최선을 다하고 있습니다.
  ▶ We're trying _____ _____ to make this website a valuable asset for our customers.

C Refer to the Korean and fill in the blanks.

1 You should complete it _____ _____ as you can.
  할 수 있는 한 빨리 그것을 끝내야 해요.

2 Could you let me know the _____ of the contract with CJ?
  CJ와의 계약 상황을 알려주시겠어요?

3 _____ do you think the blog update will be _____?
  블로그 업데이트가 언제 끝날 것 같아요?

4 We are running _____ _____ _____ to come up with new solutions.
  새로운 해결책을 찾기에는 시간이 없어요.

5 How _____ along are you in your analysis?
  당신이 맡은 분석은 어디까지 진행됐어요?

37.mp3

A Jane, **¹have you finished** the sales report yet?

B It's almost done. But **²I'm still working on** the sales figures for the second half of the year.

A I understand that they're due today.

B I know, but I've been busy writing a budget proposal. Can you give me two more days? I'll do my best to finish them by Thursday.

A We have a board meeting on Friday. **³We're supposed to report** the sales performance there. I'll need a final copy by then.

B Understood. Don't worry about that, sir.

Pattern Training

1 Have you finished [＿＿＿＿＿＿]? ~을 끝냈나요?

① looking over chapter 2 of the report
② preparing for the presentation
③ entering all the data yet

▶ 보고서 2장 검토 / 발표 준비 / 모든 데이터 입력

2 I'm still working on [＿＿＿＿＿＿]. ~을 여전히 작업 중입니다.

① the final version of the site
② some minor changes in translation
③ updating the programs

▶ 그 사이트의 마지막 버전 / 번역에서 몇 가지 사소한 교정 / 프로그램 업데이트

3 We're supposed to report [＿＿＿＿＿＿]. ~을 보고하기로 되어 있습니다.

① our marketing plans for next year
② potential problems relating to our part suppliers
③ the current status of the project

▶ 내년 마케팅 계획 / 부품 공급업체들과 관련된 잠재적인 문제점들 / 프로젝트의 현 상황

38.mp3

A When do you think our new website will have all the problems worked out?

B **¹We're aiming for** early November. However, it may be sooner or slightly later than that.

A If we could have it up and running by the end of November, that would be great.

B Linking the website to our sponsors' banners has been a lot more difficult than we had anticipated. But we're almost there.

A As you might know, we have a big meeting with some new clients on the first day of December. And **²things would be a lot easier if** we could have access to our new website.

B Of course, I know it's absolutely important to impress our new clients. We're trying our best. The website **³is our main priority** right now.

Pattern Training

1 **We're aiming for** [＿＿＿＿＿＿]**.** ~을 목표로 하고 있습니다.

① the summer of 2023
② the first half of 2025
③ March 30
▶ 2023년 여름 / 2025년 상반기 / 3월 30일

2 **Things would be a lot easier if** [＿＿＿＿＿＿]**.** ~라면 상황은 더 쉬워질 겁니다.

① our employers made reasonable efforts
② we could figure out how to solve that problem
③ he got a laptop to bring along so he could do image editing
▶ 우리의 고용주들이 합리적인 노력을 한다 / 그 문제의 해결 방법을 찾는다 / 이미지 편집을 할 수 있게 그가 가지고 다닐 노트북이 있다

3 [＿＿＿＿＿＿] **is our main priority.** ~이 최우선 사항입니다.

① Customer privacy
② The quality of service to our customers
③ The success of your website
▶ 고객의 사생활 보호 / 우리 고객에 대한 서비스 품질 / 귀사의 웹사이트 성공

A   Complete the short dialogs with the given words.

on	fast	complete	best
by	over	sure	take

1   A: Have you finished looking _____ the report yet?

    B: Not yet. It's going to _____ one or two more days.

    보고서 검토 끝났나요? – 아직이요. 하루 이틀 더 걸릴 것 같아요.

2   A: So when will it be finished?

    B: I'll do my _____ to finish it _____ Tuesday morning.

    그거 언제 끝나겠습니까? – 화요일 오전까지 끝내도록 노력하겠습니다.

3   A: You're working overtime these days, aren't you?

    B: I have to _____ the proposal as _____ as I can.

    요즘 야근하고 계시네요, 그렇죠? – 가능한 한 빨리 제안서를 완성해야 하거든요.

4   A: Are you _____ we can get this done _____ time?

    B: Of course. Trust me.

    이것을 제때 끝마칠 수 있는 거 확실해요? – 물론이죠. 저를 믿어주세요.

B   Put the Korean into English and complete the dialogs.

1

A: How's the marketing survey coming along?

B: 거의 다 됐습니다. (it / done) We're expecting to get the results next month.

A: Next month? Come on, David. Based on the survey results, we're planning to start developing the product from early next month.

B: 저희는 최선을 다하고 있습니다. (do / best) However, getting precise feedback from customers is not as easy as we had thought.

A: Anyways, 적어도 이달 말까지 끝내주세요. (finish / at the latest)

2

A: Jeff, 보고서는 얼마나 진척되었어요? (how far along ...?)

B: I have completed the preliminary review and analyzed the data, and I am almost done writing the analytical review.

A: That's great. 일정보다 앞서 있는 것 같군요. (look like / ahead) When you are done, send it to me to review.

B: I'll send it to you Monday morning. That should give you a day to review it.

A: That's great. Keep up the good work.

A Listen to the dialog and answer the questions.

39.mp3

1 What is Michael's problem?

▶

2 Where was Michael supposed to be?

▶

3 What did Michael do this morning?

▶

4 Who most likely is Lisa?

▶ Michael's

B Listen again and complete the blanks.

39.mp3

Lisa: Michael, I ____¹____ _____ _____ _____ _____ London to work on the project. What happened?

Michael: I didn't realize my visa had expired!

Lisa: Shame on you! Don't you know ²____ _____ _____ _____ _____?

Michael: I know, Lisa. I ³____ _____ _____ _____ of my visa this morning.

Lisa: When do you think ⁴____ _____ _____ _____?

Michael: I'm aiming for early next week. However, it ⁵____ _____ _____ _____ than that.

Lisa: Do whatever is needed to ⁶____ _____ _____ _____ _____!

C Listen to the dialog and check true or false.

40.mp3

	True	False
1 Jeremy had knee surgery.		
2 Jeremy is in charge of writing the product specifications.		
3 Jeremy will come back to work next week.		
4 The woman wants to have the meeting earlier.		

문제에 대한 논의 및 해결

Discussing and Solving Problems

Vocabulary & Expressions

문제 보고하기

- **raise an error** 오류를 일으키다
- **cause a problem** 문제를 일으키다
- **We have a problem with** ~에 문제가 있습니다
- **There is a problem with** ~에 문제가 있네요
- **We have some trouble with** ~와 문제가 좀 생겼습니다
- **The problem is closely related to** 문제는 ~와 밀접하게 연관되어 있어요
- **The problem has something to do with** 문제는 ~와 관련 있습니다
- **We believe the problem resulted from** 문제는 ~에서 발생했다고 봅니다
- **The problem resulted in** 그 문제는 ~한 결과를 초래했습니다

문제 해결책 논의하기

- **technical glitch** 기술적인 결함
- **find out the root cause** 근본적인 원인을 알아내다
- **investigate** 조사하다, 연구하다
- **restore** 복구하다
- **get to repair work** 복구 공사에 착수하다
- **work out / solve / settle** 해결하다
- **solution** 해결책

문제 해결책 제시하기

- **How about ...? / Why don't you ...?** ~하는 게 어때요?
- **We should / We need to / We have to** 우리는 ~해야 해요
- **If I were you, I'd** 내가 당신이라면 ~하겠어요
- **I'd suggest** ~하기를 제안합니다
- **Make sure that** ~을 확실하게 하세요

Useful Expressions

- Has this problem been reported previously? 이 문제가 전에 보고된 적이 있나요?
- It's starting to get on my nerves. 그게 슬슬 제 신경을 건드리고 있어요.
- I can't get the server to work. 서버를 작동시킬 수가 없어요.
- We never heard about this problem. 이 문제에 대해서 들어본 적이 없어요.
- The current version is working fine with no problem at all. 현재 버전은 아무 문제 없이 잘 작동하고 있어요.

A Match the meanings on the left with the expressions on the right.

1 기술적인 결함 ·   · ⓐ complaint

2 때때로, 가끔 ·   · ⓑ technical glitch

3 결함 있는 제품 ·   · ⓒ defective product

4 불만사항 ·   · ⓓ root cause

5 근본적인 원인 ·   · ⓔ at times

B Fill in the blanks with the given words.

1 메일 서버에 문제가 좀 있었습니다.
  ▶ We had some _____ _____ the mail server.

2 이 문제는 어제 제가 보고했던 버그와 밀접하게 연관되어 있습니다.
  ▶ This problem is closely _____ _____ the bug which I reported yesterday.

3 그 문제는 이 기계의 소프트웨어와 관련이 있습니다.
  ▶ The problem has something to _____ _____ the software on this machine.

4 그 문제를 해결하기 위한 회의를 소집합시다.
  ▶ Let's call a meeting to _____ _____ the problem.

5 그 일이 앞으로 다시는 발생하지 않도록 확실하게 하세요.
  ▶ _____ _____ that doesn't happen again in the future.

Words
related to
work out
make sure
trouble with
do with

C Refer to the Korean and fill in the blanks.

1 Has anyone come up with a _____ to the problem?
  그 문제에 대한 해결책을 갖고 있는 사람 있어요?

2 _____ this kind of malfunction been _____ before?
  이러한 종류의 오작동이 전에 보고된 적이 있나요?

3 I don't think the problem _____ _____ hacking or a computer virus.
  저는 그 문제가 해킹이나 컴퓨터 바이러스에서 기인했다고 생각하지 않습니다.

4 We need to _____ all the possibilities we can use.
  우리가 이용할 수 있는 모든 가능성들을 조사해봐야 합니다.

5 Be sure to check out the _____ _____ of June's sales loss and tackle it with the right methods.
  6월분 판매 손실의 근본 원인을 조사하고 알맞은 방법으로 해결하도록 하세요.

41.mp3

A Felix, [1]**we received a complaint** from a customer.

B Really? Could you explain it in detail?

A She bought one of our speakers about a week ago. It works fine. But at times, there's a loud, high-pitched sound that plays for a few seconds and then goes away. She said it really hurts her ears.

B Hmm… Has this problem been reported by anyone previously?

A [2]**We never heard about** this technical glitch before.

B What does she want? Does she want a refund, or does she want to exchange it?

A She wants a refund.

B Get the defective speaker back and [3]**find out the root cause** so it won't happen again in the future.

Pattern Training

1 **We received a complaint** [_____]. ~ 불만을 접수했습니다.

① from an employee at Alpha Airlines
② about the way we deal with our customers
③ that we have posted copyright-protected material on our website without the owner's authorization

▶ 알파 항공사의 한 직원으로부터 / 우리가 고객들을 다루는 방식에 대해 / 우리가 저작권 보호를 받는 자료를 소유권자의 승인 없이 우리 웹사이트에 올렸다는

2 **We never heard about** [_____]. ~에 대해서 들어본 적이 없어요.

① anything like that before
② this noise problem until now
③ any trouble completing the online application

▶ 전에 그와 같은 것 / 지금까지 이 소음 문제 / 온라인 지원서를 작성할 때 어떠한 문제

3 **Find out the root cause of** [_____]. ~의 근본적인 원인을 밝혀내세요.

① this fiasco
② the failure before corrective action can be taken
③ the problem so we can send an error report to the Internet service provider

▶ 이 대실패 / 수정 조치를 취하기 전에 그 실패 / 인터넷 서비스 업체에게 오류 보고서를 보낼 수 있도록 그 문제

42.mp3

A We tried everything, but ¹**we just can't get** the firewall **to work**. At first, we thought it was a problem with the software installed. But look at this. The software is working absolutely fine.

B Did you install the patch program?

A Of course. We did that according to the user's manual.

B Then what's the problem?

A It's starting to get on my nerves. ²**My concern is that** somebody might hack into our Intranet.

B ³**Why don't you** just wait and try calling an IT security company tomorrow morning? I'm sure they'll send a technician to help us if needed.

A Yeah. I think that's the only thing we can do at this point.

Pattern Training

1   **We just can't get** [＿＿＿＿＿＿] **to work.** ~을 작동시킬 수가 없어요.

① the wireless system
② the washing machine we bought yesterday
③ the digital camera
▶ 무선 시스템 / 어제 우리가 산 세탁기 / 디지털 카메라

2   **My concern is that** [＿＿＿＿＿＿]. 제 걱정은 ~라는 것입니다.

① they actually own the copyright
② we have a meeting with a producer next Monday
③ my boss may have taken a disliking to me
▶ 사실상 그들이 저작권을 가지고 있다는 / 다음 주 월요일에 제작자와 회의가 있다는 / 상사가 저를 싫어했을지도 모른다는

3   **Why don't you** [＿＿＿＿＿＿]? ~하는 것이 어떨까요?

① go in to see him and say you're sorry
② invite them to a high-class restaurant
③ skim the contract on the flight back from Paris
▶ 그를 찾아가서 미안하다고 하는 / 그들을 고급 식당으로 초대하는 / 파리에서 돌아오는 비행기편에서 계약서를 검토하는

A   Find the correct responses to complete the dialogs.

1   Has this heat problem been reported before?

2   Why don't we call an emergency meeting?

3   We found some technical glitches.

4   Did the problem result from unrealistic expectations?

5   I can't get the printer to work.

6   Did you find out why it's not working properly?

> **Responses**
> ⓐ What's wrong with it?
> ⓑ Nope, we're still investigating the root cause of the malfunction.
> ⓒ Yes, our expectations are too high.
> ⓓ No, we never heard about that before.
> ⓔ Yeah, I think it's a good idea.
> ⓕ I hope they aren't too serious.

B   Put the Korean into English and complete the dialogs.

1

A: 우리 고객 중 한 분으로부터 불만을 접수했어요. (receive / a complaint)

B: What's the problem?

A: He said the wireless mouse he bought isn't working.

B: 그건 배터리랑 관련 있을 것 같은데요. (have something to do with)
Please have him check the batteries.

A: The batteries were fully charged.

B: Then, please get it back and 문제의 근본 원인을 알아내세요. (find out)

2

A: I hate the computer system here! The server's down yet again.

B: 왜 서버에 문제가 있다고 생각하는 거죠? (What makes ...? / have a problem)

A: I can't check my email. It comes up with an error saying that it couldn't connect to the server.

B: That's weird. I'm online right now, and I'm checking my email without a problem. Perhaps you should call the Technical Support Center and 그들 중 한 사람이 당신의 컴퓨터를 살펴보게 하세요. (have *someone* take a look at)

Practice 2 — Listen-up!

A Listen to the dialog and check true or false.

43.mp3

	True	False
1 Mr. Brasher got stuck in heavy traffic.		
2 Mr. Brasher is supposed to report on the traffic conditions.		
3 The speakers will receive the documents by courier service.		

B Listen again and complete the blanks.

43.mp3

Kevin: Mr. Brasher just called and said he's __¹____ _____ _____ _____ now.

Rachel: No way! __²____ _____ _____ _____ go over our presentation with him.

         How long did he say it __³____ _____ _____ _____ _____ ?

Kevin: He said he __⁴____ _____ _____ _____ _____ _____ to the

         meeting considering the traffic conditions. Why don't we start without him?

Rachel: My concern is that he has all the documents __⁵____ _____ _____ _____ .

         I don't know what to do.

Kevin: __⁶____ _____ _____ _____ to send the documents by email?

Rachel: That's a good idea.

C Listen to the dialog and answer the questions.

44.mp3

1 What is the problem?

▸ _____

2 What will happen if the blueprints aren't ready by Tuesday?

▸ _____

3 What is the speakers' alternative plan?

▸ _____

4 Why can't Molly work on the weekend?

▸ _____

스트레스 관리 및 자기계발

Controlling Stress and Self-improvement

Vocabulary & Expressions

스트레스 관련 어휘

- **be stressed out** 스트레스로 지치다
- **be under stress[pressure]** 스트레스를 받다
- **feel a lot of stress** 스트레스를 많이 받다
- **put pressure on** ~에게 압력을 가하다
- **reduce[relieve] stress** 스트레스를 줄이다[풀다]
- **get rid of stress by -ing** ~함으로써 스트레스를 해소하다

스트레스 해소법

- **think positively** 긍정적으로 생각하다
- **get enough sleep** 충분한 수면을 취하다
- **get exercise** 운동하다
- **stretch out** 스트레칭을 하다
- **be buried in meditation** 명상에 잠기다

자기 계발과 건강 관리

- **self-improvement** 자기 계발
- **pick up useful working skills** 유용한 업무 기술을 습득하다
- **learn a foreign language** 외국어를 배우다
- **eat right** 제대로 먹다
- **be on a diet to keep fit** 건강 유지를 위해 식이요법을 하다
- **exercise regularly** 규칙적으로 운동하다
- **I'm learning ... on a regular basis.** ~을 정기적으로 배우고 있습니다.
- **I'm taking a class in** ~ 수업을 듣고 있습니다
- **I make it a rule to** ~하는 것을 규칙으로 삼고 있습니다

🔵 Plus Vocabulary 스트레스의 증상

- **irritability or anger** 짜증 또는 분노
- **apathy or depression** 무관심 또는 우울
- **constant anxiety** 지속적인 불안
- **loss of appetite** 식욕 부진
- **increased smoking** 흡연량 증가
- **drinking** 음주
- **excessive tiredness** 극도의 피곤
- **stomach problems** 위장 질환

Useful Expressions

- This decision makes us more stressed.
  이번 결정이 우리를 **더 스트레스 받게 만드네요**.
- This incentive program will keep us motivated.
  이 인센티브 제도가 우리에게 **동기를 유발해줄** 겁니다.
- They are running a training program for their workers.
  그들은 직원들을 위한 훈련 **프로그램을 운영하고 있어요**.
- How do you take care of your health?
  당신은 어떻게 **건강을 챙깁니까**?
- My company trains us to pick up a new language.
  우리 회사는 직원들이 새로운 **언어를 배우도록 교육시킵니다**.

A Match the meanings on the left with the expressions on the right.

1 사업을 확장하다   •   • ⓐ energetic

2 자기 계발   •   • ⓑ expand one's business

3 사업 환경   •   • ⓒ run a program

4 열정적인   •   • ⓓ business environment

5 프로그램을 운영하다   •   • ⓔ self-improvement

B Fill in the blanks using the given words.

1 그는 현재 업무량이 많아서 스트레스로 많이 지쳐 있습니다.
   ▶ He has a heavy workload at the moment and is very _____ _____.

2 내 상사는 지속적인 구조조정 때문에 스트레스를 받고 있어요.
   ▶ My boss is _____ _____ because of the constant reorganization.

3 지난 4개월간 정기적으로 체육관에 갔어요.
   ▶ I've spent the last 4 months attending a gym on a _____ _____.

4 내 상사는 계속해서 일요일에 일하도록 나에게 압력을 넣고 있어요.
   ▶ My supervisor _____ _____ me to work on Sunday.

5 어떤 방법으로 스트레스를 해소하세요?
   ▶ How do you _____ _____ of stress?

Words
get rid
under stress
regular basis
stressed out
keep pressuring

C Refer to the Korean and fill in the blanks.

1 I'm on a _____ to keep myself _____.
   건강 유지를 위해 식이요법을 하고 있어요.

2 I _____ it a _____ to study English every day for an hour.
   저는 매일 한 시간씩 영어 공부하는 것을 규칙으로 삼고 있습니다.

3 I'm taking a _____ in _____ to work with our Spanish partners more efficiently.
   스페인 파트너들과 좀 더 효율적으로 일하기 위해서 스페인어 수업을 듣고 있습니다.

4 If you eat right and _____ _____, you will lose weight.
   제대로 먹고 규칙적으로 운동한다면 몸무게를 줄일 수 있습니다.

5 My boss _____ his stress _____ taking his frustrations out on his subordinates.
   내 상사는 자기 욕구불만을 부하 직원들에게 발산함으로써 스트레스를 풉니다.

45.mp3

A   [1]**He's pressuring** me to finish the report by tomorrow. I can't stand his attitude!

B   Take it easy, Cindy. Pressure is part of all work and helps to [2]**keep us motivated**.

A   But he's such a go-getter that he's bothering everybody else around him. It seems like he does not know that everybody is trying to get away from him.

B   Yeah, I know. He acts like he's always right and only his opinion matters. However, I heard that excessive pressure can lead to stress, which undermines performance.

A   No doubt about it. Hey, Todd, let's stop talking about it. It [3]**makes me more stressed**.

Pattern Training

1   **He is pressuring** _____ . 그는 ~하라고 압력을 넣고 있어요.

① me to act faster
② everyone in the office into setting him up with a date
③ vendors to make these technologies more reliable

▶ 내게 좀 더 빨리 움직이라고 / 사무실에 있는 모든 사람에게 데이트를 추천해 달라고 / 업체들에게 이 기술을 좀 더 믿을 만하게 만들라고

2   _____ **keep(s) us motivated.** ~은 우리에게 동기 유발을 해줍니다.

① Goals
② Your suggestions and contributions
③ Positive thinking

▶ 목표 / 당신의 제안과 공헌 / 긍정적인 생각

3   _____ **makes me more stressed.** ~이 더욱 스트레스 받게 만듭니다.

① Learning Chinese
② Working overtime every single night
③ Working with him on a team

▶ 중국어를 배우는 것 / 매일 밤 초과 근무하는 것 / 한 팀에서 그와 함께 일하는 것

Conversation 2 | Self-improvement and health care 자기 계발과 건강 관리

46.mp3

A Did you hear ¹**the company is going to run** a training program for self-improvement in the workplace?

B Really? That sounds interesting. What are we supposed to learn?

A Management is planning to expand our business abroad next year. So ²**they want to train us to** pick up English, especially for the business environment. We're supposed to complete an e-learning module.

B I think that's a good idea. E-learning makes it possible for us to learn anywhere at anytime.

A Yeah. By the way, I heard that you've been working overtime every day. ³**How do you take care of** your health?

B Actually, I wake up at 5 in the morning and go to the company health club. I usually exercise one hour a day before I go to the office. That keeps me energetic.

Pattern Training

1 **The company is going to run** ⌐‒‒‒‒‒‒‒‒‒‒‒‒‒‒‒¬. 회사가 ~을 운영할 것입니다.

① an incentive program
② a training program for our resellers across the country
③ a marketing campaign to sell our e-books

▶ 인센티브 프로그램 / 전국의 재판매업자들을 대상으로 교육 프로그램 / 전자책 판매를 위한 마케팅 캠페인

2 **They want to train us to** ⌐‒‒‒‒‒‒‒‒‒‒‒¬. 그들은 우리가 ~하도록 교육시키고자 합니다.

① think logically
② know how to use polite language in the workplace
③ see what is significant and what is not

▶ 논리적으로 생각하도록 / 직장 내에서 예의 바른 언어 사용법을 알도록 / 무엇이 중요하고 무엇이 중요하지 않은지 판단하도록

3 **How do you take care of** ⌐‒‒‒‒‒‒‒‒‒‒¬? ~을 어떻게 관리하세요?

① your stress and anxiety
② your everyday expenses
③ the operating costs of this website

▶ 당신의 스트레스와 불안 / 당신의 일상 경비 / 이 웹사이트의 운영 비용

A Make sentences using the given words.

put pressure on / get ... done	make it possible / pick up
keep pressuring *someone* to	on a regular basis / work efficiency

1 이 프로그램은 우리가 새로운 기술을 빨리 습득할 수 있게 해줍니다.

▶ _____

2 그는 내가 병가를 내지 못하도록 계속해서 압력을 가하고 있어요.

▶ _____

3 그는 우리가 일을 더 빨리 끝내도록 압력을 넣었어요.

▶ _____

4 우리는 직원들의 업무 효율 향상을 위해 정기적으로 워크숍을 엽니다.

▶ _____

B Put the Korean into English and complete the dialogs.

1

A: You are smoking more frequently. 요즘 스트레스 받고 있어요? (stressed out)

B: The deadline is coming up soon. But things aren't turning out as I had planned.

A: 맑은 공기를 마시며, 스트레칭을 해보지 그래요? (enjoy the fresh air / stretch out) It would relieve your stress.

B: That's a good idea. Thank you for the tip.

2

A: What do you do after work?

B: 헬스클럽에서 한 시간 가량 운동해요. (exercise / a health club) It makes me feel good.

A: Wow! I didn't know that.

B: And then, 집에서 인터넷으로 중국어를 배워요. (learn / online) Our company is opening a new branch office in China, and I'll be the head of it.

A: I see. You deserve it. You are one of the hardest workers at this company.

A   Listen to the dialog and check true or false.   47.mp3

	True	False
1 The speakers are mainly talking about their boss.		
2 The man has to work overtime to finish something.		
3 The woman is suggesting having a drink.		
4 Breathing is good for eliminating stress according to the woman.		

B   Listen again and complete the blanks.   47.mp3

Josh: How can I _¹_____ _____ from my life?

Emily: Why? What's up with you?

Josh: My boss _²_____ _____ _____ to work overtime until my job is finished.

He's acting like a dictator. Tell me how I can _³_____ _____ _____?

Emily: I feel sorry for you, Josh. You should learn to _⁴_____ _____ _____

_____ to stress. Slow, deep breathing will bring your respiration back to normal.

_⁵_____ _____ _____ _____. Give it a go, man.

Josh: No, I just fancy a drink.

C   Listen to the dialog and answer the questions.   48.mp3

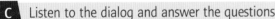

1 What are they talking about?

   ⓐ company restructuring

   ⓑ the features of Microsoft Word

   ⓒ where to learn the features of Microsoft Excel

2 Where is Rachel transferring to?

   ⓐ the Personnel Department   ⓑ the Sales Department

   ⓒ the Advertising Department   ⓓ the Accounting Department

3 What will probably happen next?

   ⓐ The speakers will learn some good manners.

   ⓑ Rachel will visit a website.

   ⓒ Rachel will meet the members of her new department.

Michael Eisner
"Golden Retriever"

The Walt Disney Company is one of the largest media and entertainment corporations [1] **on earth.** Disney's primary production facilities, as well as its headquarters, are currently located in Burbank, California.

Michael D. Eisner was its CEO from September 22, 1984, to September 30, 2005. When Disney did poorly in the late '90s, he was penalized with no annual bonus. But he [2] **managed to bag** an $11.5 million reward for fiscal 2000 [3] **thanks** largely to his smart investment in ABC's *Who Wants To Be A Millionaire.* He also boosted Disney's profits six-fold and sent its share price soaring almost 6,000%.

Described as creative and energetic, Eisner helped steer Disney out of a two-year [4] **financial slump.** Eisner is used to these [5] **ups and downs** when it comes to both the company and his compensation. As one of the world's highest compensated CEOs, Eisner [6] **set a world record** in December 1997 by exercising $570 million in stock options. Also, don't forget that this is the man who built Paramount into a leading studio during the 1970s until he joined Disney.

© Jonathan Weiss/shutterstock

© George sheldon/shutterstock

월트 디즈니 사는 지구 상에서 가장 큰 미디어 엔터테인먼트 회사 중 하나다. 디즈니 본사뿐 아니라 주요 생산 시설들은 현재 캘리포니아 주 버뱅크에 위치해 있다.
마이클 D. 아이스너는 1984년 9월 22일부터 2005년 9월 30일까지 이 회사의 CEO였다. 90년대 후반 디즈니의 실적이 형편없었을 때, 아이스너는 연간 보너스를 받지 않는 페널티를 받았다. 그러나 2000년 회계연도에는 ABC 방송국의 '누가 백만장자가 되고 싶은가' 프로그램에 현명하게 투자한 덕에 1천1백5십만 달러를 간신히 챙기게 되었다. 그는 또한 디즈니의 수익을 6배 증가시켰으며 주가를 거의 6천 퍼센트나 치솟게 했다.
창조적이고 열정적인 사람으로 대변되는 아이스너는 디즈니를 2년 간의 재정적인 슬럼프에서 구출했다. 아이스너는 회사와 자신의 보수에 관해 흥망성쇠 관리의 달인이다. 세계에서 가장 많은 봉급을 받는 CEO 중 한 명으로, 아이스너는 1997년 12월에 스톡옵션으로 5억7천만 달러를 행사함으로써 세계기록을 세웠다. 또한, 이 사람이 디즈니에 입사하기 전까지 1970년대에 파라마운트를 선도적인 영화사로 만들어낸 바로 그 사람이라는 사실을 잊지 말라.

1 **on earth** 세상에서, 지구 상에서

Come and enjoy the greatest show **on earth**!
지상 최대의 쇼를 보러 오십시오!

2 **manage to** (간신히) ~해내다

Within ten minutes, Mr. McGuinty had **managed to** engage his boss in conversation.
10분 안에 맥귄티 씨는 그의 상사가 대화에 끼어들도록 간신히 유도해냈다.

3 **thanks to** ~덕분에

Thanks to its millions of customers, eNatural was able to conduct high-quality research.
수백 만의 고객 덕분에 이내츄럴은 최고의 연구를 수행할 수 있었다.

© spiderman777/shutterstock

4 **financial slump** 재정적인 어려움

Only time will tell if Apson will be able to rise above its current **financial slump**.
앱손이 현재의 재정적인 어려움을 극복할지는 오로지 시간이 말해줄 것이다.

5 **ups and downs** 흥망성쇠, 오르내림

Your mix of investments should allow you to stay ahead during the **ups and downs** of the stock market.
당신의 투자 분산은 주식 시장의 등락 중에도 항상 앞서가도록 해줄 겁니다.

6 **set a world record** 세계 기록을 세우다

A 32-year-old Singaporean man **set a world record** for holding his breath.
32살의 싱가포르 남자가 숨 참기 세계 기록을 세웠다.

Who is Michael Eisner?

1942년 3월 뉴욕 생으로 1984~2005년 디즈니의 CEO이다. 그가 파라마운트 영화사의 사장 겸 COO를 그만둔 직후 디즈니의 CEO로 지목되었을 당시, 디즈니 사는 문제가 많은 소규모 애니메이션 제작과 테마 유원지 사업을 하는 기업일 뿐이었다. 그러나 지난 20년간 아이스너는 기업 자산가치를 약 30억 달러에서 700억 달러를 호가하는 수준으로 성장시킴으로써 디즈니 최고의 전성기를 가져왔다. 그는 골든 리트리버라고 불릴 만큼 한번 온 기회는 놓치지 않고 성공으로 이끄는 달인이다.

© Joe Seer/shutterstock

Michael Eisner says...

"If it's not growing, it's going to die."
성장하지 않으면 죽는다.

"It is rare to find a business partner who is selfless. If you are lucky, it happens once in a lifetime."
남을 생각해주는 비즈니스 파트너를 만나는 것은 드문 일이다. 운이 좋다면 일생에 한 번 정도 만나겠지.

"My strength is coming up with two outs in the last of the ninth."
나의 진짜 실력은 9회 말 투 아웃 후에 나온다.

Practical Business
Expressing Opinions Effectively

PART 4
효과적인 의사 표현

의견 교환 및 상호 신뢰

Exchanging Opinions and Mutual Trust

Vocabulary & Expressions

의견 강조하기

- **It is little wonder that** ~라는 것은 당연합니다, ~은 이상할 것이 없습니다
- **It's not too much to say that** ~라고 말해도 과언이 아닙니다
- **There is some reason to think that** ~라고 생각하는 데도 일리가 있습니다
- **There can be no doubt that** ~라는 데는 의심의 여지가 없습니다

반어적으로 표현하기

- **Can it be true?** 그게 사실이겠어요?
  - → **It cannot be true.** 그게 사실일 리가 없어요.
- **Who knows where he is?** 그가 어디에 있는지 누가 알겠어요?
  - → **Nobody knows where he is.** 아무도 그가 어디에 있는지 몰라요.
- **Who doesn't love his family?** 누가 자기 가족을 사랑하지 않겠어요?
  - → **Everyone loves his family.** 누구나 자기 가족을 사랑합니다.

🔲 Plus Tip

부정의문문과 긍정의문문

긍정의 내용을 강조하기 위해 부정의문문으로 묻고, 부정의 내용을 강조하기 위해 긍정의문문으로 묻기도 하는데, 이는 대답을 요구하는 것이 아니라 듣는 이를 납득시키기 위해 반어적으로 표현하는 것이다.

신뢰와 믿음 표현하기

- **I understand your position, but** 당신의 입장을 이해합니다만,
- **Of course I know your situation pretty well now, but** 물론 당신의 상황을 잘 알고 있습니다만,
- **I'll trust in you and put ... under your control.** 당신을 믿고 ~을 당신 관리 하에 맡길게요.
- **We rely[depend] on you to** 당신이 ~해주실 것을 믿어요
- **I have full confidence in** ~을 확신합니다

Useful Expressions

- Who wants to be demoted or lose a job?
- I can't believe you've done this to me.
- You deserve a pay raise.
- It is bad timing to come out with something like this.
- Any relationship should be based on trust and respect.

누가 좌천되거나 일자리를 잃기 **원하겠어요?**

당신이 내게 이런 짓을 했다니 **믿을 수가 없군요.**

당신은 봉급을 올려 받을 만합니다.

이런 걸 내놓는 **것은 시기적으로 좋지 않아요.**

모든 관계는 신뢰와 존중을 **바탕으로 해야 합니다.**

A Match the meanings on the left with the expressions on the right.

1 경영진 ·   · ⓐ operating manual

2 재정 문제 ·   · ⓑ management

3 파업에 들어가다 ·   · ⓒ a pay raise

4 사용 설명서 ·   · ⓓ financial problem

5 임금 인상 ·   · ⓔ go on strike

B Fill in the blanks with the given words.

Words
no doubt
understand
some reason
too much
little wonder
position

1 당신 입장은 이해하지만 당신이 요청하는 것은 비현실적이에요.
   ▶ I _____ your _____, but what you are asking is unrealistic.

2 많은 직원들이 화가 난 것은 당연합니다.
   ▶ It is _____ _____ that many workers are infuriated.

3 프로젝트 지연이 발생할 것이라고 생각하는 데도 일리가 있습니다.
   ▶ There is _____ _____ to think that a project delay will occur.

4 회사의 미래가 지도자들에게 달려 있다고 해도 과언이 아닙니다.
   ▶ It's not _____ _____ to say that the company's future depends on its leaders.

5 그 문제를 오직 당신만이 해결할 수 있다는 데 의심의 여지가 없습니다.
   ▶ There can be _____ _____ that the problem can only be resolved by you.

C Refer to the Korean and fill in the blanks.

1 I'll _____ in you and put the Personnel Department _____ your control.
   당신을 믿고 인사과를 당신의 관리 하에 맡기겠습니다.

2 We _____ on you to _____ us to deliver the most effective service.
   우리가 가장 효과적인 서비스를 제공하도록 당신이 도와주실 것이라고 믿어요.

3 We have full _____ in his leadership.
   우리는 그의 지도력을 확신합니다.

4 Who wouldn't want a high salary? = _____ _____ a high salary.
   누가 고액 봉급을 원치 않겠어요? = 누구나 고액의 봉급을 원합니다.

5 Who knows he was an industrial spy? = _____ _____ he was an industrial spy.
   누가 그가 산업 스파이였다는 것을 알겠어요? = 아무도 그가 산업 스파이였다는 것을 몰라요.

49.mp3

A As a customer, I really love being treated in a special way. When I go into a store, I want a staff member to politely open the door for me.

B That's what all customers want. ¹**Who wants to** be treated badly?

A Financially ailing companies usually have bad customer service.

B Absolutely. But our company just focuses on the products and making money. ²**It's little wonder that** we are losing our customers to the competition.

A ³**How can** management **possibly not know** that great service brings more customers? I can't believe that we are still making our customers read operating manuals. We need to patiently explain how to use our products over the phone.

Pattern Training

1 **Who wants to** [_____]**?** 누가 ~하는 것을 원하겠어요?

① help her get a job
② spend weekends working on a project
③ be homeless

▶ 그녀가 일자리를 구하도록 돕는 / 프로젝트를 작업하며 주말을 보내는 / 노숙자가 되는

2 **It's little wonder that** [_____]**.** ~은 이상한 일이 아니에요.

① they experience difficulties
② few companies are making a profit these days
③ the team has accomplished this quarter's sales goal

▶ 그들이 어려움을 겪고 있는 것 / 요즘 흑자를 내는 회사가 거의 없다는 것 / 그 팀이 이번 분기 매출 목표를 달성했다는 것

3 **How can** [_____] **possibly not know** [_____]**?**
어떻게 …가 ~을 모를 수가 있죠?

① they, how to use it
② he, the answer to that simple question
③ she, the role of the second secretaries

▶ 그들, 그것의 사용법 / 그 남자, 그 간단한 질문에 대한 답 / 그 여자, 보조 비서의 역할

50.mp3

A How did the negotiations go?

B We did not agree to a new contract in the end. We want to receive more pay. So we are thinking about going on strike.

A [1]**I know that** you guys deserve it. However, isn't it too hard for management to accept your demands? Our company is ailing from a severely devalued stock price. [2]**It's bad timing to** talk about a pay raise.

B I know. So we told them we'd like to renegotiate after we solve the financial problem together. Because we know our relationship [3]**should be based on trust and respect** for each other.

Pattern Training

1　**I know that** [_____]. ~을 알고 있습니다.

① you won't let me down
② I couldn't have done it without them
③ it's hard to make it

▶ 당신이 나를 실망시키지 않을 것이라는 사실 / 그들 없이는 그것을 해내지 못 했을 것이라는 것 / 해내기 어렵다는 것

2　**It's bad timing to** [_____]. ~하기에 시기가 안 좋습니다.

① raise these issues
② hire more mechanical engineers
③ release software when hardware is in short supply

▶ 이 문제점들을 거론하기에 / 기계 기사를 더 고용하기에 / 하드웨어 공급이 부족한 때에 소프트웨어를 출시하기에

3　[_____] **should be based on trust and respect.**
~은 신뢰와 존중에 바탕을 두어야 합니다.

① The partnership
② Our relationship
③ Building relationships with co-workers

▶ 파트너십 / 우리 관계 / 동료들과 관계를 형성하는 것

Practice 1   Let's Speak!

A   Complete the short dialogs with the given words.

possibly	go	wonder	bad
how	timing	well	little

1   A: It's _____ _____ that they are asking for a bigger company parking lot.

    B: Absolutely.

    그들이 더 큰 회사 주차장을 요구하는 것은 당연해요. – 동감입니다.

2   A: _____ can you _____ not know that you're transferring to the Sales Department?

    B: No one has told me about it.

    당신이 영업부로 옮길 것이라는 것을 어떻게 모를 수가 있죠? – 아무도 얘기해주지 않았어요.

3   A: It's _____ _____ to talk about our working environments.

    B: I think this issue also should be discussed urgently.

    우리 근무 환경에 대해서 말하는 것이 시기적으로 좋지 않습니다. – 이 문제 또한 시급히 논의되어야 한다고 생각해요.

4   A: How did the meeting _____?

    B: It went _____.

    회의는 어땠어요? – 잘 됐어요.

B   Put the Korean into English and complete the dialogs.

1

A: 우리가 아직도 타자기를 사용하고 있다니 믿을 수가 없어. (believe / typewriter)
How can management possibly not know the importance of office equipment for work efficiency?

B: That's what I'm saying. Maybe we should bring this up at the next staff meeting.

2

A: We've decided to fire David.

B: What's the matter?
항상 그를 믿고 중요한 프로젝트들을 맡겨왔는데요. (trust in / leave ... to someone)

A: I heard the news that he's been stealing our confidential documents.

B: I can't believe it!

A　Listen to the dialog and answer the questions.　51.mp3

1 What are the speakers mainly talking about?
ⓐ the reputation of their company
ⓑ the company logo samples

2 Who designed the company logo samples?
ⓐ the woman
ⓑ the man
ⓒ a design company

3 What is the man's opinion about the green-colored logo?
ⓐ It is eye-catching.
ⓑ It is ill-matched.

B　Listen to the dialog and check true or false.　52.mp3

	True	False
1 Mr. Thomson is supposed to give the budget projections to Emma by Wednesday.		
2 Linda is already finished with the budget projections.		
3 Mr. Thomson is complaining about Linda's laziness.		
4 Mr. Thomson trusts Linda.		

C　Listen again and complete the blanks.　52.mp3

Thomson: Linda, ¹＿＿＿ ＿＿＿ ＿＿＿ ＿＿＿ the budget projections?

Linda:　I'm not. I'm still working on them. When do you need them by, Mr. Thomson?

Thomson: I'll need them ²＿＿＿ ＿＿＿ ＿＿＿ ＿＿＿ ＿＿＿ so I can give them to Emma by Wednesday.

Linda:　Don't worry. I'm almost finished.

Thomson: I ³＿＿＿ ＿＿＿＿ ＿＿＿. You know, I always thank you for the sweet things you've done for me, Linda.

Linda:　Don't mention it, Mr. Thomson. Actually, I'd ⁴＿＿＿ ＿＿＿ ＿＿＿ ＿＿＿ ＿＿＿ always trusting me.

WEEK 11

추측과 확신 및 불평과 이해

Guessing and Convincing & Complaining and Understanding

Vocabulary & Expressions

추측하기

- **It seems / It appears / It looks** ~인 것 같습니다, ~인 것처럼 보입니다
- **It sounds** ~인 것 같습니다, ~인 것처럼 들립니다
- **It is likely to** ~할 것 같습니다
- **It is unlikely to** ~할 것 같지 않습니다
- **I guess / I suppose / I think** ~라고 짐작합니다
- **It may be / It might be** ~일지도 모릅니다

확신하기

- **I'm sure that** ~라는 것을 확신합니다
- **I firmly believe that** ~라는 것을 굳게 믿습니다
- **I can say with confidence** ~을 자신 있게 말할 수 있습니다
- **I'm confident[convinced] that** ~라는 것을 확신합니다
- **It is clear[obvious] that** ~라는 점이 분명합니다

불평하기

- **complain about / grumble about** ~에 대해 불평하다
- **be unfair** 불공평하다
- **stand / put up with** ~을 견디다, ~을 참다
- **I'm unhappy with** ~이 불만족스러워요
- **I'm sick and tired of / I'm fed up with**
  ~에 질렸어요, ~이 지긋지긋해요
- **I'm annoyed by** ~으로 인해 성가십니다
  (= I'm bothered by, I'm troubled by)
- **I have a problem with** ~에 애로점이 있어요

이해하기

- **I got it. / I get your point.**
  무슨 말인지 알겠어요.
- **I understand what you mean.**
  무슨 말씀인지 이해합니다.
- **It makes sense to me.**
  이해가 가는군요.
- **I see what you're getting at.**
  무슨 말씀인지 알겠습니다.

Useful Expressions

- We've got to take action.
  조치를 취해야 **합니다.**
- I'm sick and tired of people sitting around doing nothing.
  가만히 앉아서 아무 일도 안 하는 사람들이 **지긋지긋합니다.**
- That's what you think.
  그건 당신 **생각이지요.**
- At times, we need to ask for some legal advice.
  때로는 법률 상담을 요구할 필요가 있어요.
- I'm not sure when the new prices go into effect.
  언제부터 새로운 가격이 적용될지 **모르겠어요.**

Vocabulary Check-Up

A Match the meanings on the left with the expressions on the right.

1 ~에 갇혀 있다 ·

2 병에 걸리다 ·

3 식중독 ·

4 공개 사과 ·

5 전력 차단 ·

· ⓐ get sick

· ⓑ electricity cutoffs

· ⓒ a public apology

· ⓓ food poisoning

· ⓔ be stuck in

B Fill in the blanks with the given words.

Words
might
believe
obvious
firmly
sure
unlikely

1 그 목표들은 달성될 수 없을 것이 분명합니다.
▶ It is _____ that the goals cannot be reached.

2 우리가 위기 상황에 놓인 게 확실합니다.
▶ I'm _____ that we are in a crisis situation.

3 그 제품을 올해가 아니라 내년에 출시하는 것이 현명한 일일지도 모릅니다.
▶ It _____ be wise to launch the product next year, not this year.

4 프로젝트 납기일을 맞출 수 없을 것 같습니다.
▶ It is _____ that we can meet the project deadline.

5 저는 직장에서 성희롱을 몰아낼 수 있다고 굳게 믿습니다.
▶ I _____ _____ that we can drive sexual harassment out of the workplace.

C Refer to the Korean and fill in the blanks.

1 I can _____ with _____ that our business plan will pay off.
우리의 사업 계획이 결실을 맺을 것이라는 점을 자신 있게 말씀드릴 수 있습니다.

2 I am beginning to get _____ _____ _____ the work.
이제 그 일에 신물이 나려고 해요.

3 I _____ what you're _____ at.
무슨 말씀하시는지 알겠어요.

4 He always _____ about his lack of time.
그는 항상 시간이 부족하다고 불평해요.

5 That makes perfect _____ to me.
완벽히 이해가 가는군요.

53.mp3

A People got sick after eating our sandwiches.

B Unbelievable! **¹We've been watching out for** food poisoning, haven't we?

A Yeah, but there seems to have been some problem with the peanut butter. Some of the peanut butter must have been spoiled due to the electricity cutoffs from the flood.

B How could this happen? This could ruin the company's reputation.

A **²I'm not sure when** this trouble would be on the news, but we've got to take action to minimize the damage.

B Do you have any good ideas?

A **³I firmly believe that** we have to issue a public apology immediately.

Pattern Training

1 **We've been watching out for** [_____].

~을 주의해 왔습니다.

① something like this for some time
② what our workers eat
③ each other for so long

▶ 일정 기간 이러한 것 / 우리 직원들이 섭취하는 것 / 오랫동안 서로

◯ 유사 표현

▸ **We've been keeping an eye on** improvements in digital imaging for many years.
우리는 수년간 디지털 이미징의 발전**을 주목해 왔습니다.**

2 **I'm not sure when** [_____]. 언제 ~할지 모르겠습니다.

① a good time to reopen the store is
② we should carry out the new marketing plan
③ he'll return to work

▶ 매장을 다시 여는 것이 좋을지 / 새 마케팅 계획을 실행해야 할지 / 그가 업무에 복귀할지

3 **I firmly believe that** [_____]. ~라고 확신합니다.

① these relationships will last a lifetime
② our workers are what make us special
③ the development of our teams' diversity is key for the business to move forward

▶ 이러한 관계가 평생 지속될 것이라고 / 우리 직원들이야말로 우리를 특별하게 만들어준다고 / 우리 팀의 다양성 개발이 사업을 발전시키는 열쇠라고

54.mp3

A **¹I'm sick and tired of** being stuck in the office all day! Look at my boss. He always goes out for dinner with clients.

B Well, Justin, I do not want to tell you this, but the executives have more stress.

A That's what you think, Olivia. They have company cars and do not have to work late at night. Moreover, their salaries are a lot higher than ours.

B However, **²at times, we need to understand that** they always have to make important decisions. Besides, **³they have to take care of** their team members, which makes them stressed out as well.

A I still think this is unfair.

Pattern Training

1 I'm sick and tired of [_____]. ~이 지긋지긋합니다.

① working all night long
② my same old daily routine
③ making my boss happy

▶ 밤새도록 일하는 것 / 만날 똑같은 일만 하는 것 / 상사를 기쁘게 해주는 것

2 At times, we need to understand that [_____]. 때론 ~을 이해할 필요가 있습니다.

① we are living in a hierarchical system
② their pensions are more generous than ours
③ there are many different corporate cultures

▶ 우리가 위계 체제에 살고 있다는 것 / 그들의 연금이 우리 연금보다 더 많다는 것 / 다양한 회사 문화가 있다는 것

3 They have to take care of [_____]. 그들은 ~에 신경을 써야 해요.

① organizing the convention
② the progress on the projects
③ all the problems facing our company right now

▶ 대회를 조직하는 것 / 프로젝트의 진행상황 / 지금 우리 회사가 직면한 모든 문제들

A Complete the short dialogs with the given words.

times	like	convinced	stand

1 A: Who do you think will win the bid?

   B: I'm _____ that we'll win the contract in the end.

     누가 입찰을 따낼 것 같아요? – 결국 우리가 그 계약을 따낼 것이라고 확신합니다.

2 A: I don't know how to prioritize my tasks.

   B: It sounds _____ you need some help with time management.

     업무의 우선순위 정하는 법을 모르겠어요. – 시간 관리하는 데 도움이 필요한 것처럼 들리네요.

3 A: I can't _____ that noise from the next building any more.

   B: Calm down. Someone said that the construction will be completed today.

     더 이상 옆 건물에서 나는 저 소음을 참을 수가 없어요. – 진정해요. 오늘 공사가 끝날 거래요.

4 A: His ideas always conflict with mine.

   B: However, at _____, you need to express that you're following his opinion.

     항상 그 사람과 난 생각이 부딪혀요. – 하지만 때로는 그 사람 의견을 따르고 있다는 것도 표현할 필요가 있어요.

B Put the Korean into English and complete the dialogs.

1

A: What do you think of Mr. Roger Ebert as a potential sales manager?

B: If he takes the position, 그는 오래 머물지 못할 것 같은데요. (I don't think / be likely to)

A: Why do you think so?

   저는 그가 잘 운영해내리라 굳게 믿는걸요. (firmly believe / manage well)

   He's been working for this company for quite a long time.

B: However, he's never been involved in sales-related work before.

2

A: I can't put up with Steve. His report is full of mistakes.

B: 일이 많아서 어찌할 바를 모르는 것 같더군요. (It looks like / be overwhelmed by) You need to understand him. Besides, he's new here.

A: 무슨 말인지 알겠어요 (understand / mean), but he's been making too many mistakes.

A Listen to the dialog and check true or false. 55.mp3

	True	False
1 Their company is planning to buy another company.		
2 Their company is financially stable at the moment.		
3 The speakers have the same opinion on the company's future.		

B Listen again and complete the blanks. 55.mp3

Hailey: At the rate we're going, ¹_____ _____ _____ _____ we're going to have a much bigger company.

Joshua: You've got it all wrong. ²_____ _____ _____ in the red.

Hailey: I'm really ³_____ _____ _____ _____ your pessimism! What makes you think that?

Joshua: As you know, our company is not financially sound at the moment. ⁴_____ _____ _____ _____ _____ another company with financial problems while we are in trouble? ⁵_____ _____ _____ ruin our company.

Hailey: Don't fret, Joshua. ⁶_____ _____ _____ that we could generate synergy by acquiring it.

Joshua: You're not listening to me, Hailey.

C Listen to the dialog and answer the questions. 56.mp3

1 Who's Chris?
ⓐ a secretary
ⓑ a marketing manager
ⓒ a sales representative
ⓓ a sales manager

2 How long has Chris been working at his current company?
ⓐ one year
ⓑ two years
ⓒ three years
ⓓ four years

직원 평가 및 직무와 책임

Evaluating Workers & Jobs and Responsibilities

Vocabulary & Expressions

직원의 성격

- **demanding** 요구사항이 많은
- **meticulous** 꼼꼼한
- **creative** 창조적인
- **friendly** 다정한
- **competitive** 경쟁심이 강한
- **organized** 체계적인
- **picky** 까다로운
- **artistic** 예술적인
- **easy-going** 태평스러운
- **hard-working** 부지런한
- **strict** 엄격한

직원 평가하기

- **judge by** ~으로 판단하다
- **misjudge** 잘못 판단하다
- **think highly of** *someone* ~를 높이 평가하다
- **give** *someone* **too much credit**
  ~를 과대평가하다 (= overrate *someone*)
- **underestimate** 과소평가하다
- **conduct job assessments** 직무 평가를 실시하다
- **performance evaluation** 실적 평가
- **I think / I believe** ~라고 생각합니다

책임과 의무 표현하기

- **be responsible for / be in charge of** ~을 담당하다, ~을 책임지다
- **take the blame for** ~에 대한 비난을 받다, ~에 대해 책임지다
- **have a strong sense of responsibility** 책임감이 강하다
- **I will take care of / I will take on** 제가 ~을 맡겠습니다
- **I will handle ... on my own.** 제 힘으로 ~을 처리하겠습니다.
- **You should accept your responsibility as** 당신은 ~으로서의 책임을 받아들여야 합니다
- **You must / You have to / You've got to / You need to** 당신은 ~해야 합니다
- **You're supposed to** 당신은 ~하기로 되어 있습니다

Useful Expressions

- He always wants to finish his work as late as possible.
  그는 **언제나** 자신의 일을 가능한 한 늦게 끝내려고 **합니다**.

- He should take the blame.
  그가 **비난을 받아야** 합니다.

- He is not as smart as his co-workers.
  그는 자기 동료들만큼 영리하지 않아요.

- It's your job to secure a network.
  네트워크를 안전하게 관리**하는 게 당신 업무입니다**.

- I didn't expect to learn from my boss.
  내 상사한테 배울 **거라고는 생각 못했어요**.

A Match the meanings on the left with the expressions on the right.

1 경쟁심이 강한 ·

2 실적 평가 ·

3 잘못 판단하다 ·

4 안일한, 태평스러운 ·

5 실수를 저지르다 ·

· ⓐ performance evaluation

· ⓑ competitive

· ⓒ easy-going

· ⓓ make a mistake

· ⓔ misjudge

B Fill in the blanks with the given words.

1 당신은 오늘 저녁 9시에 연설하기로 되어 있습니다.
  ▶ You're _____ to give a speech at 9 tonight.

2 제가 직접 전체 프로젝트를 처리하겠습니다.
  ▶ I will _____ the entire project on my own.

3 당신은 이 프로젝트에 참여해야 해요.
  ▶ You _____ _____ to take part in this project.

4 다른 사람이 합류한다면 그 일을 맡겠습니다.
  ▶ I will _____ _____ the job if someone else joins me.

5 그가 열심히 일하지 않는다는 것이 아니라 팀플레이어가 아니라는 것입니다.
  ▶ It's not that he's not _____, but he's not a team player.

> **Words**
> have got
> hard-working
> supposed
> take on
> handle

C Refer to the Korean and fill in the blanks.

1 I'll _____ _____ of your work while you're away.
  당신이 없는 동안 제가 당신의 일을 처리하겠습니다.

2 Who should _____ _____ _____ for falling sales?
  누가 매출 감소에 대한 책임을 저야 할까요?

3 We _____ that he is very knowledgeable.
  우리는 그가 아주 박식하다고 생각합니다.

4 We've been giving her too _____ _____.
  그녀를 너무 과대평가해 왔어요.

5 He's in _____ _____ making all the key decisions about the marketing program.
  그는 마케팅 프로그램에 관한 모든 주요 사항들을 결정하는 것을 담당하고 있습니다.

57.mp3

A So, you've been a manager for 6 months. How are you finding it working here?

B The work is great and professional. But **¹I didn't expect to** have a problem with my junior staff. Mostly, it's William.

A Isn't he smart?

B It's not that he's not smart, but he's not a team player. **²He always wants to do things** on his own way.

A How about Kenny?

B **³He is not as** smart **as** William. But he is really organized and knows how to work together as a team. I'm thinking about transferring William to some other work not involving a team effort.

Pattern Training

1   **I didn't expect to** ☐☐☐. ~할 거라고 예상하지 못했습니다.

① get promoted so quickly
② have too much difficulty
③ stay so long at this company

▶ 그렇게 빨리 승진될 / 그렇게 많은 어려움이 있을 / 이 회사에 그렇게 오래 있을

2   **He always wants to do things** ☐☐☐. 그는 모든 일을 ~하게 하기 원합니다.

① by himself
② thoroughly
③ smarter, not harder

▶ 혼자서 / 철저하게 / 열심히 하지 않고 영리하게

3   **He is not as** ☐☐☐ **as** ☐☐☐. 그는 …만큼 ~하지는 않아요.

① dumb, we first thought
② dedicated, he needs to be to actually complete his goals
③ responsible for the consequences, Hippler

▶ 우리가 처음 생각한 것만큼 멍청하지는 / 목적을 달성하기 위해 필요한 만큼 헌신적이지는 / 히플러만큼 결과에 책임감을 갖지는

58.mp3

A We got a complaint from a customer named John Rowe.
He said we sent a bill for a shipment that he never received.
What's wrong, Fred?

B **¹I have no idea** where that problem came from.
Let me check and get back to you. … Nancy,
²I just found out that Diana made a mistake.

A That is the third time this year, you know. **³You should
take responsibility for** it since you are the manager of
the Shipping Department. It's your job to check your staff
members' daily work.

B Yes, I should take the blame. I will educate my staff so that
they will realize the importance of their work.

Pattern Training

1 **I have no idea** [_____]. ~을 모르겠어요.

① why Mr. Ridell resigned
② when they'll really finish it
③ how to work on a team of designers

▶ 리델 씨가 사임한 이유 / 그들이 정말 언제 그것을 끝낼지 / 디자이너 팀에서 일하는 법

🔵 강조 표현

· **I haven't the faintest idea** what
you're talking about.
도대체 무슨 말씀을 하시는지 **도통 모르겠어요.**

· **It beats me** how he managed to
finish the report within a day.
그가 어떻게 하루만에 보고서를 완성했는지
도통 모르겠네요.

2 **I just found out that** [_____]. ~을 알아냈습니다.

① he called me this morning
② he is well suited for this job
③ we had a fire in our warehouse last night

▶ 그가 오늘 아침에 내게 전화했다는 것 / 그가 이 일에 제격이라는 것 / 지난 밤에 우리 창고에 불이 났다는 것

3 **You should take responsibility for** [_____]. 당신은 ~에 책임져야 합니다.

① your wrongdoings
② your organization's performance
③ the fiasco that happened last month

▶ 당신의 잘못된 행동 / 당신 조직의 성과 / 지난 달에 발생한 비참한 결과

Practice 1 / Let's Speak!

A Make sentences using the given words.

expect / become close to	take the blame	do things / thoroughly
accept responsibility	organized / meticulous	be responsible for / inventory status

1 당신 행동에 책임을 져야 합니다.

▶ _____

2 제가 팀원들과 그렇게 가까워질 줄은 예상하지 못했어요.

▶ _____

3 당신은 인사과 부장으로서 책임을 받아들여야 합니다.

▶ _____

4 그는 매일 재고 현황 확인하는 것을 책임지고 있습니다.

▶ _____

5 제 상사는 언제나 일 처리를 철저하게 하길 원합니다.

▶ _____

6 그녀는 샐리만큼 체계적이거나 꼼꼼하지 않아요.

▶ _____

B Find the correct responses to complete the dialogs.

1 You should take responsibility for the failure.

2 How about the new-comer Susan?

3 Do you mean he is very demanding and strict?

4 How do you like your work?

5 We received a complaint from a healthcare professional.

> **Responses**
> ⓐ She is kind of a go-getter.
> ⓑ Yes, I should take the blame.
> ⓒ What happened?
> ⓓ It's very challenging.
> ⓔ It's not that he's demanding, but he doesn't know how to get along with his co-workers.

A Listen to the dialog and check true or false.   59.mp3

	True	False
1 Alicia does not like her boss.		
2 Kevin is making good money.		
3 Kevin and his boss communicate without any problems.		
4 Kevin's boss might be fired.		

B Listen again and complete the blanks.   59.mp3

Kevin: I'm at my wit's end, Alicia.

Alicia: You have a great job. You are ___¹___ _____ _____. Kevin, what's the problem?

Kevin: Here's my problem. I ___²___ _____ _____ _____, and I'm quite sure he feels the same way about me. We ___³___ _____ _____, and he is always criticizing me.

Alicia: Yeah, I know he is very ___⁴___ _____ _____.

Kevin: You can say that again. In addition, he is ___⁵___ _____ _____.

Alicia: I heard that our executives are thinking of firing him. So don't worry, Kevin.

C Listen to the dialog and answer the questions.   60.mp3

1 Jordan thinks Kelly is [_____] her job.

2 Kelly has to prepare the [_____] [_____] for the weekly meeting.

3 Kelly missed the [_____] that Jordan sent.

+ BIZ TIPs   당신은 어떤 직원?

go-getter 야망이 큰 사람

all-around nice guy 다방면에서 잘 어울리는 사람

hell-raiser 목소리만 큰 문제 직원

closer 상황 마무리를 잘하는 사람

go-to man 문제가 있을 때 찾아가면 답을 얻을 수 있는 사람

wonder boy 상사의 총애를 얻은 유능한 젊은 직원

young Turk 젊고 능력도 있는 야심가

backstabber 뒤에서 찌르는 사람, 배신자

greenhorn 머리에 피도 안 마른 신입사원

반박과 호응 및 다양한 삽입어

Refuting and Responding Favorably & Interpolating

Vocabulary & Expressions

반박하기

- **That's out of the question.** 그건 불가능해요.
- **It doesn't make sense.** 말이 안 돼요.
- **I see things differently.** 전 다르게 생각합니다.
- **You've got it all wrong.** 완전히 잘못 알고 있군요.
- **I wouldn't say that.** 전 그렇게 말하고 싶지 않아요.
- **That has nothing to do with it.** 그건 이것과 관련이 없어요.
- **That's beside the point.** 요지에서 벗어났어요.
- **That's what you think.** 그건 당신 생각이죠.

호응하기

- **You can say that again.** 내 말이 그 말이에요.
- **You said it.** 당연한 말씀이에요.
- **I'm with you.** 동감입니다.
- **That's for sure.** 맞아요.
- **You bet.** 틀림없어요.(내기를 걸어도 좋아요.)
- **I can relate to what you're saying.** 그 말에 공감합니다.
- **I hear you.** 동감합니다.
- **You've got a point there.** 일리가 있네요.

추가하기

- **additionally** 게다가
- **also** 또한
- **as well as** ~뿐만 아니라
- **besides** 게다가
- **furthermore** 뿐만 아니라
- **in addition** 게다가
- **what's more** 덧붙여서

대조 및 비교하기

- **although** ~이긴 하지만
- **despite** ~임에도 불구하고
- **nevertheless** 그럼에도 불구하고
- **however** 그러나
- **on the other hand** 한편, 반면에
- **whereas** 반면에
- **while** ~하는 반면
- **in the same way / similarly / likewise** 비슷하게, 마찬가지로

도입하기

- **first of all** 우선
- **by the way** 그건 그렇고
- **regarding** ~에 관하여
- **speaking of** ~에 관해 말한다면

조건 나타내기

- **as far as** ~하는 한
- **in case** ~의 경우
- **only if** ~할 경우에 한해

강조하기

- **in any event** 어떤 경우에도
- **in fact** 사실은
- **particularly / especially** 특히
- **indeed** 확실히

예외 나타내기

- **aside from** ~을 제외하고
- **except for** ~을 제외하고
- **unless** ~하지 않는 한

Useful Expressions

- That's ridiculous! — 터무니없군요!
- How are things going? — 일은 어떻게 되어가고 있어요?
- How often do you update our website? — 웹사이트를 얼마나 자주 업데이트하죠?
- It's definitely worth a read. — 정말로 읽을 만합니다.
- I'd say 10% of people use it. — 10%의 사람들이 그것을 사용한다고 말하고 싶군요.

Vocabulary Check-Up

A Match the meanings on the left with the expressions on the right.

1 비슷하게 ·   · ⓐ conduct a survey

2 조사를 실시하다 ·   · ⓑ similarly

3 특히 ·   · ⓒ negative

4 전원 코드 ·   · ⓓ particularly

5 부정적인 ·   · ⓔ power cord

B Fill in the blanks using the given words.

1 그것은 우리의 환불 정책과 아무런 관련이 없어요.
  ▶ That _____ _____ to do with our return policy.

2 TV 광고에 7만 달러를 투자하는 것은 저에겐 말이 안 돼요.
  ▶ It doesn't _____ _____ to me to invest $70,000 in a TV commercial.

3 주가에 대한 말씀에 공감합니다.
  ▶ I _____ _____ to what you're saying about our stock prices.

4 저는 상황을 다르게 보고 있습니다.
  ▶ I see things _____.

5 게다가, 그녀는 상점의 총괄책임자로 승진될 겁니다.
  ▶ _____ _____, she will get promoted to general manager of a store.

> **Words**
> make sense
> in addition
> differently
> can relate
> have nothing

C Refer to the Korean and fill in the blanks.

1 _____ _____ _____, please make sure you have the presentation ready by June 13.
  그건 그렇고, 6월 13일까지 발표 준비를 확실하게 완료하세요.

2 On the _____ _____, we have to be prepared for any potential emergency.
  한편, 우리는 발생 가능성 있는 비상 상황에 대비해야 합니다.

3 Keep your office space looking good, _____ your desk.
  사무실 공간을 보기 좋게 유지하세요. 특히 당신 책상 말이에요.

4 I bet you can't find anyone _____ Sarah Silverman as a marketing manager.
  마케팅 부장으로 사라 실버맨 같은 사람은 찾을 수 없을 거라고 장담합니다.

5 _____ _____ as I know, they are almost done with the report.
  제가 아는 한, 그들은 보고서를 거의 끝냈습니다.

Conversation 1　Refuting　반박하기

61.mp3

A We're planning to make a notebook without a battery.

B That's ridiculous. **¹I don't care** what you guys are doing. You always come up with weird ideas.

A **²I'm pretty convinced that** this is going to be a huge hit!

B You have conducted a customer survey, haven't you? Users definitely need a battery so that they can use their laptops without power cords.

A Well, they also want cheaper notebooks.

B Oh, come on! So do you think they want to remove an essential feature to reduce the price?

A **³Why are you so negative about** everything that has to do with my product planning team?

B I'm not negative about your team, just their ideas.

Pattern Training

1　**I don't care** [_____]. 저는 ~을 상관 안 해요.

① how much people hate me
② when the ordered goods get here
③ why you need this confidential information

▶ 사람들이 얼마나 나를 싫어하는지 / 주문품이 언제 여기에 도착하는지 / 왜 당신이 이 기밀 정보를 필요로 하는지

2　**I'm pretty convinced that** [_____]. ~라고 확신합니다.

① this is a great opportunity
② we can make big money out of the booming education industry
③ the business plan must be prepared under faculty supervision

▶ 이것이 좋은 기회라고 / 크게 일고 있는 교육산업에서 큰 돈을 벌 수 있다고 / 사업 계획은 임원들의 감독 하에 준비되어야 한다고

3　**Why are you so negative about** [_____]?

왜 ~에 대해 그렇게 부정적이에요?

① Ms. Tina Ballard
② our healthcare system
③ every point we make

▶ 티나 밸라드 씨 / 우리 건강관리 시스템 / 우리가 지적하는 모든 점

More Expressions

부정적인 사람 묘사하기

▸ He is always **concerned about** the consequences of his work.
그는 언제나 그의 업무 결과를 **걱정한다.**

긍정적인 사람 묘사하기

▸ He always **looks on the bright side** of things.
그는 언제나 상황의 **긍정적인 면을 본다.**

62.mp3

A Jeff, I heard we're bidding for the one-billion dollar deal.

B Right. I think [1]**we have an edge** because we have competitive pricing.

A I feel the same way. [2]**By the way**, how often do you take clients out to eat?

B I'd say about two times a month on average. Why?

A Our executives think we are spending too much money treating our clients.

B But it's definitely worth it. In fact, I clinched a multi-billion dollar deal with a dot-com company a week ago.

A Then, I guess it's worth it.

B [3]**Besides**, they will be visiting next week to discuss another advertising contract.

Pattern Training

1 **We have an edge** ⸻. 우리는 ~ 유리한 점이 있습니다.

① over our competitors

② which makes us different and stand out

③ because we are introducing a new fuel-efficient engine

▶ 우리 경쟁자들보다 / 우리를 남다르게 구별되게 하는 / 연료 효율이 좋은 새로운 엔진을 도입하기 때문에

2 **By the way,** ⸻**?** 그건 그렇고, ~?

① did you meet with the clients yesterday

② how long do you think it would take to download the files

③ do we need to diversify our investments to lower our risks

▶ 어제 고객들 만났어요? / 그 파일들을 다운받는 데 얼마나 걸릴 것 같아요? / 위험을 줄이기 위해 투자를 분산시킬 필요가 있을까요?

3 **Besides,** ⸻**.** 게다가, ~.

① we should open a new sales office in Beirut

② we can make our mistakes on paper

③ I wrote a report for the board of directors last night

▶ 베이루트에 새로운 영업사무소를 열어야 합니다 / 우리가 실수한 것을 문서로 정리할 수 있습니다 / 어젯밤에 이사회에 낼 보고서를 썼어요

Practice 1 \ Let's Speak!

A Complete the short dialogs with the given words.

attractive	say	break	differently
expand	sure	build	point

1 A: I think we should _____ our business slowly and carefully.

   B: I see things _____.

천천히 조심스럽게 사업을 확장해야 한다고 생각해요. – 전 다르게 생각하는데요.

2 A: We need to _____ and promote our own website.

   B: That's for _____. That could also be a communication window with our customers.

우리만의 웹사이트를 만들어서 홍보할 필요가 있어요. – 맞아요. 고객과의 대화 창구도 될 수 있고요.

3 A: We should let line workers take a _____ every hour.

   B: I wouldn't _____ that because it's against company policy.

생산직 직원들이 매 시간 쉬도록 해줘야 합니다. – 전 그렇게 생각하지 않아요. 왜냐하면 그건 회사 정책에 위배되거든요.

4 A: The current prices of our smartphones aren't _____.

   B: You've got a _____ there.

우리 스마트폰의 현재 가격은 구미가 당기지 않아요. – 일리가 있는 말입니다.

B Make sentences using the given words.

as long as	in fact	besides
even though	by the way	unless

1 사실, 그는 회사의 판매 계획에 부정적입니다. (negative / sales plan)

   ▶ _____

2 새 것인데도 불구하고, 이 계산기는 제대로 작동하지 않아요. (calculator / function properly)

   ▶ _____

3 게다가, 이 서비스는 많은 시간과 돈을 절약해줍니다. (save / a lot of)

   ▶ _____

4 비가 오지 않는 한 우리는 세미나를 개최할 겁니다. (hold / rain)

   ▶ _____

5 그건 그렇고, 우리가 왜 시장점유율을 잃고 있는 거죠? (lose / market share)

   ▶ _____

6 당신이 우리 팀에 속해 있는 한, 우리 팀의 방침을 따라야 해요. (be on one's team / follow the policy)

   ▶ _____

A   Listen to the dialog and answer the questions.   63.mp3

1   What are the speakers talking about?

    ⓐ their winter vacation

    ⓑ buying a mobile phone

    ⓒ the launch date of a product

    ⓓ their favorite phones

2   When does Logan think a peak period for buying mobile phones is?

    ▶ _____

B   Listen again and complete the blanks.   63.mp3

Logan: Can I __¹_____ _____ _____ _____ _____, Katharina?

Katharina: Sure. What's up, Logan?

Logan: We must decide the date of the launch __²_____ _____ _____ _____.

    When are we going to launch the Smartphone?

Katharina: Personally, I'm __³_____ _____ _____ September.

Logan: __⁴_____ _____ _____ till the winter?

Katharina: Why wait any longer?

Logan: It's a peak period for buying mobile phones.

Katharina: It __⁵_____ _____ _____ _____ _____. Why should we have to

    wait another three months? Let's just cash in on that __⁶_____ _____ _____

    _____.

C   Listen to the dialog and check true or false.   64.mp3

	True	False
1 The speakers are talking about selling products offline.		
2 Lisa wants to have the website ready within a month.		
3 One of the keys to success is providing quality information.		
4 The website completion is being delayed by Lisa.		

Sam Walton
"Economy of Scale"

Sam Walton, [1]**along with** his brother Bud Walton, co-founded the world's largest retail chain, Wal-Mart, on July 2, 1962. His strong marketing skills and attention to detail led to Wal-Mart's expansion [2]**throughout** the United States.

By 1990, Wal-Mart was the nation's top retailer [3]**in terms of** sales, and Walton was one of the richest men in the world.

Sam [4]**took a** closer **look at** an overlooked market segment: small-town America. He would look for deserted farmland equidistant from three towns. The small-town residents were already used to traveling many miles to get their groceries, so the distance was no [5]**obstacle**.

In addition, Sam accomplished this feat largely through economy of scale: As production increases, the cost of producing each additional unit falls. And the bigger Wal-Mart got, the larger its profit margins became.

© Thomas Dutour/shutterstock

© Ken Wolter/shutterstock

샘 월튼은 1962년 7월 2일 그의 형제 버드 월튼과 함께 세계에서 가장 큰 유통 체인 월마트를 창립했다. 그의 빼어난 마케팅 역량과 세심함으로 월마트는 미국 전역으로 번져나가게 되었다. 1990년까지 월마트는 매출 면에서 미국에서 가장 큰 유통업체였고, 월튼은 세계에서 가장 부유한 사람 중 하나가 되었다.
샘은 간과되었던 시장인 미국의 작은 마을들을 자세히 들여다보았다. 그는 세 개의 마을에서 같은 거리에 위치한 인적이 없는 농장을 찾았다. 그 마을 주민들은 이미 식품을 사려고 수십 마일쯤은 거뜬히 이동하는 데 익숙해져 있었다. 그래서 거리는 장애가 되지 않았다.
게다가, 샘은 주로 규모의 경제를 이용하여 이 업적을 성취했다. 생산량이 늘면 하나 더 생산하는 데 드는 비용이 줄어든다. 그리고 월마트가 더 커질수록 그들의 이윤은 더 늘어났다.

1 along with ~ ~와 함께

I, **along with** 25,000 other people, protested against imports of cheap American beef.

2만5천 명의 사람들과 함께, 나는 값싼 미국 소고기 수입에 반대하여 시위했다.

2 throughout ~전역에 걸쳐

They conducted a survey **throughout** the city.

그들은 그 도시 전역에 걸쳐 여론 조사를 실시했다.

3 in terms of ~면에서

This company ranked the highest **in terms of** customer satisfaction.

이 회사가 고객만족도 면에서 1위에 올랐다.

4 take a look at ~을 들여다보다

Please **take a** closer **look at** the bar graph on the screen.

화면에 있는 막대그래프를 자세히 봐주세요.

5 obstacle 장애물

I want to learn how to overcome **obstacles** in life.

인생의 장애물을 극복하는 법을 배우고 싶다.

© Quality HD/shutterstock

Who is Sam Walton?

1918년 3월 29일 오클라호마 생. 1930년 경제 대공황을 거쳐 1940년에 미주리 대학(the University of Missouri)을 졸업했다. 그가 1962년에 설립한 월마트는 백화점 중심의 소매 유통산업을 근본적으로 바꾼 것은 물론, 유통이 제조보다 우위에 서게 함으로써 전세계 소비자들이 최저가에 제품을 소비할 수 있는 소비자 중심 사회를 견인한 공로를 인정받고 있다. 이 성과에 힘입어 샘 월튼은 1998년 타임이 뽑은 20세기 가장 영향력 있는 인물 100명에 선정되었으며, 월마트는 경제지 포춘 지가 선정한 '미국에서 가장 존경받는 기업'에 2003, 2004년 연속으로 뽑혔다.

Sam Walton says...

"Capital isn't scare; vision is."

부족한 것은 자본이 아니다. 비전이다.

"Outstanding leaders go out of their way to boost the self-esteem of their personnel. If people believe in themselves, it's amazing what they can accomplish."

훌륭한 리더는 직원들의 자존감을 높여준다. 사람들이 자신을 믿게 되면, 그들이 이루는 것은 가히 경이로울 뿐이다.

"High expectations are the key to everything."

높은 기대치가 모든 것의 열쇠이다.

Practical Business
Business E-mail

SPECIAL PART
비즈니스 이메일

UNIT 01

의견 묻고 나누기

Asking and Sharing Opinions

Subject	An idea for e-newsletter ————————————○ 제목
From	howard@star.com ————————————○ 보내는 사람
To	cotrain@star.com, david@star.com, hudson@star.com ——————○ 받는 사람

65.mp3

Greetings, folks. ————————○ 사내에서 돌리는 이메일이라면 캐주얼하게 써도 좋다.
Folks가 '여러분'의 뜻이 있다는 것도 잘 활용하자.

We're planning to develop an e-newsletter for our company. As we all know, it's been too difficult for us to communicate effectively because we are working in different locations in different countries. So an e-newsletter would help us know what is happening at our company. So can anyone help me out by giving me suggestions as to what content should be in the e-newsletter? I would be grateful if you could share your ideas with me.

Thanks,
Howard Cha
Software Technical Lead

제목: 전자회보에 대한 아이디어

안녕하세요, 여러분.

회사 전자회보를 개발하려고 계획 중입니다. 모두 아시다시피, 서로 여러 나라 여러 다른 지역에서 일하기 때문에 우리가 효과적으로 의사소통을 하는 것이 너무 어려웠습니다. 따라서 전자회보는 우리 회사에서 어떤 일이 일어나고 있는지 아는 데 도움이 될 것입니다. 전자회보에 어떤 콘텐츠가 들어가는 것이 좋은지 제안해서 저를 도와주실 분 계십니까? 아이디어를 저와 공유해주실 수 있다면 감사하겠습니다.

감사합니다.
하워드 차
소프트웨어 기술팀장

We are planning to develop ~을 개발할 계획입니다

We are planning to develop a new book on making effective PowerPoint presentations.

▶ 효과적인 파워포인트 발표를 만드는 것에 관한 새로운 책을 개발할 계획입니다.

It has been too difficult for us to 우리가 ~하는 것이 너무 어려웠습니다

It has been too difficult for us to sell our products in the Indonesian market.

▶ 인도네시아 시장에서 제품을 파는 것이 너무 어려웠습니다.

It would help us know 그것은 우리가 ~을 아는 데 도움이 될 것입니다

It would help us know our financial status.

▶ 그것은 우리 재정 상황을 이해하는 데 도움이 될 것입니다.

I would be grateful if you could 당신이 ~할 수 있다면 감사하겠습니다 _ 감사를 정중하게 표현하는 방법

I would be grateful if you could respond to this letter by the 2nd of July.

▶ 7월 2일까지 이 편지에 답변해주실 수 있다면 감사하겠습니다.

Vocabulary Check-Up

Fill in the blanks with the appropriate expressions.

1 우리 모두가 알다시피, 이 스마트폰에는 많은 기계적인 문제가 있습니다.

▶ _____ _____ _____ _____, this smartphone has lots of mechanical problems.

2 정해진 예산 내에서 공장을 운영하기가 너무 어려웠습니다.

▶ It has been _____ _____ _____ _____ to operate the plant within an established budget.

3 그것은 우리가 인턴들을 최대한 잘 관리하는 방법을 아는 데 도움이 될 것입니다.

▶ It _____ _____ _____ _____ how to best manage our interns.

4 몽골 시장에 관한 정보를 보내주시면 감사하겠습니다.

▶ I would be _____ _____ _____ _____ send us information on the Mongolian market.

5 우리는 새로운 노트북을 개발할 계획입니다.

▶ We are _____ _____ _____ a new laptop.

1 "당신의 의견을 알려주세요" [의견을 요청할 때]

▶ 상대방에게 의견을 요청하는 가장 전형적인 표현. opinion 대신에 thought 또는 thinking을 써도 좋다.

> **Please let me know your opinion about** the new product. It will start being developed once the detailed specifications are defined.

신상품에 대한 당신의 의견을 알려주세요. 세부 사양이 확정되면 개발이 시작될 것입니다.

2 "제 생각에는" [의견을 말할 때]

▶ 조금 캐주얼하게 말할 때는 I tell you what을 써도 좋다.

> **In my view[opinion]**, we would be much better off financially by firing unnecessary workers and closing nonproductive branches in the United States.

제 생각에는, 불필요한 인력을 해고하고 미국 내 비생산적인 지점을 철수함으로써 재정적으로 훨씬 나아질 거라 생각합니다.

3 "드릴 의견이 없습니다" [의견이 없을 때]

▶ 상대방이 의견을 원하나 의견이 없을 때도 있다. 그럴 때는 이렇게 말해보자.

> **It is difficult to comment on** the proposed regulation without seeing the specific definitions.
>
> **I don't have an opinion on** the matter.
>
> **I can't give you an opinion on** your proposal.

구체적인 정의를 보지 않고는 그 제안된 규정에 뭐라 말씀드리기 어렵습니다.
그 문제에 대해 드릴 의견이 없습니다.
당신 제안에 드릴 의견이 없어요.

4 "그 문제는 별로 중요한 것이 아닙니다" [문제가 경미함을 알릴 때]

▶ 상대방의 질문이 무의미하거나 대답할 가치가 없다고 느껴질 때에는 다음과 같이 대꾸해보자.

> Whether or not we should use this chipset **is a minor issue**.
>
> **I don't think it is important to** decide if we should hire a healthcare professional or not right now.

이 칩셋을 사용해야 하는지 아닌지는 사소한 문제입니다.
우리가 건강관리 전문가를 지금 당장 고용해야 하는지 아닌지를 결정하는 게 중요하다고 생각하지 않습니다.

Pattern Training

1 ~에 대한 당신의 의견을 알려주세요.

Please let me know your opinion about _____ .

① 매출 계획   the sales plans

② 우리의 목표를 어떻게 성취할지   how to accomplish our goal

③ 이것 중 어떤 것이 웹사이트에 더 어울리는지   which one of these is better for our website

2 제 생각에는, ~.

In my view, _____ .

① 우리는 확실히 고객 만족에 중점을 둘 필요가 있습니다   we need to keep a clear focus on customer satisfaction

② 거론된 그 공장 부지는 부적합합니다   the proposed factory site is unsuitable

③ 그는 팀에 부정적인 영향을 끼치고 있습니다   he is having a negative impact on the team

3 ~에 대해 드릴 의견이 없습니다.

I can't give you an opinion on _____ .

① 봉급을 올려달라는 당신의 요청   your request for a pay raise

② 우리 주가가 왜 떨어지는지   why our stock price is declining

③ 그 부도덕한 업체를 어떻게 다룰지   how we should deal with the unethical vendor

4 ~은 사소한 문제입니다.

_____ is a minor issue.

① 현재의 재정 상황   The current financial situation

② 제품의 기계적인 문제   The mechanical problem of the product

③ 그리스에 또 다른 지점을 둬야 할지 말지   Whether we need to have another branch in Greece

Writing Exercise

A Complete the sentences using the given words.

1 저희는 커피 맛 아이스크림을 개발할 계획입니다.
(plan / develop / coffee-flavored)

▶ _____.

2 어떤 도움도 없이 저 혼자서 이틀 안에 보고서를 완성하는 것은 어렵습니다.
(difficult / without any help / within two days)

▶ _____.

3 그것은 고객들이 우리 서비스에 대해 왜 불평하는지 아는 데 도움이 될 것입니다.
(help / know / complain about)

▶ _____.

4 그 문제에 대해 당신의 의견과 조언을 주실 수 있다면 고맙겠습니다.
(grateful / comments / advice / that matter)

▶ _____.

5 거기에 대해 모든 이가 다른 견해를 가지고 있기 때문에 이러한 종류의 상황에 대해서는 의견을 드리는 것이 어렵습니다.
(difficult / comment on / different views)

▶ _____.

6 누가 매출 감소에 책임이 있는지를 알아내는 게 중요한 것은 아니라고 생각합니다.
(I don't think / find out / sales reduction)

▶ _____.

7 누가 우리 회사의 다음 CEO가 될 것인지에 대해 드릴 의견이 없습니다.
(have an opinion / who / CEO)

▶ _____.

8 제 개인적인 견해로는, 우리는 아직 거대한 프로젝트를 맡을 준비가 되어 있지 않습니다.
(personal opinion / be ready to / take on)

▶ _____.

Refer to the Korean and complete the emails.

1   어제 회의에서 논의했듯이, 우리는 지금 새로운 내비게이션 시스템을 개발할 계획입니다. 가능한 한 빨리 당신의 의견을 알려주세요.

As we discussed at the meeting yesterday, _____ a new
navigation system. _____ as soon as possible.

2   우리 웹사이트를 현재 구축 중입니다. 여러분의 아이디어를 웹사이트에 반영할 좋은 시기라고 생각합니다. 여러분의 생각을 저와 공유
해주세요. 그러면 우리 모두가 만족하는 더 나은 웹사이트를 만들 수 있습니다.

_____. I believe this is a good time to get your
ideas on it. _____ with me so that I can make a better website
that we will be happy with.

3   당신이 작업하고 있는 웹사이트에 대해 의견을 드리기가 어렵습니다. 왜냐하면 저희는 아직 그것이 누구를 위한 것이고 어떻게 생겼는
지 정보를 받지 못했기 때문입니다. 웹사이트에 대한 구체적인 정보를 우리에게 제공해줄 수 있나요?

_____ that you are working on because
we haven't been informed of who it is for and what it looks like yet. _____
_____ on the website?

+ **TRY!**   자유롭게 이메일을 써보세요.

당신은 프로젝트 매니저로서 새롭게 시작된 프로젝트를 순조롭게 진행하기 위해 매주 한 번씩(once a week) 정기 회의(a regular meeting)
를 하고자 한다. 회의에서 논의될 주제들은 진행 상황 검토(progress review), 진행하는 데 발생한 문제점(problems), 다음 주에 할 일 등을 구
체적으로 협의하는 것이다. 따라서 프로젝트 관련자들에게 메일을 보내서 이에 대해 어떻게 생각하는지 의견을 듣고자 한다.

■ 정답은 없습니다.

동의하기 또는 반대하기

Agreeing or Disagreeing

Subject	The HappyMusic Project
From	maria@moon.com
To	mark@moon.com

66.mp3

Hello, Mark.

I agree with you that we need to hire more workers to complete the project on time. However, I don't agree at all with your suggestion that we should move the deadline back until the end of December.

I already asked our HR manger to do his best to find two or three hardware engineers. In addition, we've posted a banner saying "hardware engineers wanted" on our website.

Please keep up the good work, and I will do my part by supporting you with whatever you need.

Cheers,
Maria Young

제목: 해피뮤직 프로젝트

안녕하세요, 마크

프로젝트를 제때 끝내려면 더 많은 직원을 고용할 필요가 있다는 당신의 의견에 동의합니다. 하지만 프로젝트 마감일을 12월 말로 미뤄야 한다는 당신의 제안에는 전혀 동의할 수가 없습니다.

이미 인사과 부장에게 최선을 다해 하드웨어 엔지니어 두세 명을 더 찾아달라고 요청해 놓았습니다. 게다가, 우리 웹사이트에 '하드웨어 엔지니어 구함'이라고 쓴 배너를 올려 놓았습니다.

계속 수고해주시고, 당신이 필요한 것은 무엇이든 지원하는 데 제 몫을 다하겠습니다.

파이팅.

마리아 영

I agree with you that ~라는 당신 의견에 동의합니다

I agree with you that we should follow the company policy.

▶ 우리가 회사 정책을 따라야 한다는 당신 의견에 동의합니다.

유사 표현 **I am with you in that** ~라는 점에서 당신에게 동의합니다

I am with you in that short-term contracts increase staff turnover.

▶ 단기 계약이 직원 이직률을 증가시킨다는 점에서 당신에게 동의합니다.

I don't agree with your suggestion that ~라는 당신의 제안에 동의하지 않습니다

I don't agree with your suggestion that we should change our marketing plan.

▶ 우리의 마케팅 계획을 바꾸어야 한다는 당신의 제안에 동의하지 않아요.

move back ~을 연기하다, 미루다

I have no problem **moving back** the meeting to next Thursday afternoon.

▶ 회의를 다음 주 목요일 오후로 미루는 것에 별 문제 없습니다.

반대 표현 **bring forward** ~을 앞당기다

Can we **bring forward** the meeting from Wednesday to tomorrow?

▶ 회의를 수요일에서 내일로 앞당길 수 있을까요?

I asked ... to ~ 저는 …에게 ~을 해달라고 요청했습니다

I asked Jane **to** cancel the development project.

▶ 저는 제인에게 그 개발 프로젝트를 취소해달라고 요청했습니다.

I will do my part by ~함으로써 있어 저의 몫을 다할 겁니다 _ 자신의 역할 부분을 얘기할 때

I'll do my part by helping you overcome the obstacles.

▶ 장애물들을 극복할 수 있게 도움으로써 제 본분을 다하겠습니다.

Vocabulary Check-Up

Fill in the blanks with the appropriate expressions.

1 금요일마다 회의를 열어야 한다는 당신의 의견에 동의합니다.

▶ I _____ _____ _____ that we need to hold a meeting every Friday.

2 금융 잡지를 구독해야 한다는 당신의 제안에 동의하지 않습니다.

▶ I don't agree _____ _____ _____ that we should subscribe to a financial magazine.

3 워크숍을 목요일로 미룰 수 있을까요?

▶ Can we _____ the workshop _____ _____ Thursday?

4 점심 먹으러 가는 길이었기 때문에 상사에게 나중에 전화라고 요청했습니다.

▶ I _____ my boss to _____ _____ later because I was on my way to lunch.

5 당신에게 가장 전문적인 서비스를 제공하는 데 저의 몫을 다하겠습니다.

▶ I will _____ _____ _____ by providing you the most professional service.

Actual Sample

1 "전적으로 동의합니다" [동의를 표할 때]

▶ 강조 부사를 넣어 I wholeheartedly agree with ~로 표현할 수도 있다.

> **I am in total agreement with** your decision to build a plant there in Malaysia to deliver our goods faster. In addition, it would help us reduce our total labor costs.

우리 제품을 보다 빨리 배송하기 위해 말레이시아에 공장을 건설하겠다는 당신의 결정에 전적으로 동의합니다. 더불어, 우리의 전체 인건비를 줄이는 데 도움이 될 겁니다.

2 "동의는 합니다만" [부분적으로 동의할 때]

> **I tend to agree with your opinion, but** I also wonder if this contract could lead to increased financial strength for our company. Please let me know your opinion about my concern.

당신의 의견에 동의는 합니다만, 이 계약으로 인해 우리 회사가 재정적으로 개선될 수 있을지 또한 궁금하네요. 제 염려에 대한 당신의 생각을 알려주세요.

3 "반대하려는 것은 아니지만" [완곡하게 반대할 때]

▶ 반대를 해야 하는 경우, 상대방의 감정이 상하지 않게 완곡하게 표현하는 법도 알아두자.

> **I don't mean to disagree with you, but** I think my reasoning on this is sound. As I mentioned at the meeting last week, the most pressing issue for our company at the moment is the collapsing demand for trucks and SUVs.

반대하려는 것은 아니지만, 이 부분은 저의 논리가 맞는 것 같습니다. 지난주 회의에서 언급했듯이, 현재 우리 회사에서 가장 긴급한 문제는 트럭과 SUV의 엄청난 수요 감소입니다.

4 "~하는 것을 제안 드리고 싶습니다" [대안을 제시할 때]

▶ 상대방의 의견에 직설적으로 부정하는 대신, 곧바로 대안을 제시함으로써 부정의 뜻을 표현하는 것도 좋은 방법이다.

> **I would like to propose that** we rename our company to win more business customers, transform it into a media and content company, and bolster its digital operation.

더 많은 비즈니스 고객을 얻기 위해 회사 이름을 바꾸고, 미디어 및 콘텐츠 회사로 변경하고, 디지털 방식의 운영을 강화하는 것을 제안하고 싶습니다.

Pattern Training

1 ~라는 당신의 의견에 전적으로 동의합니다.

I am in total agreement with your opinion that ....

① 그들한테 부품을 사야 한다는   we need to buy the parts from them

② 작년에 전 세계적으로 반도체 수출이 증가했다는   worldwide sales of semiconductors grew last year

③ 그 회사를 매수하겠다는 제안을 해야 한다는   we should make an offer to purchase the company

2 당신의 의견에 동의합니다만, ~.

I tend to agree with your opinion, but ....

① 회의를 취소하는 것은 불가능합니다   it is impossible to cancel the meeting

② 그들과 좋은 관계를 유지하는 수밖에 없어요   we have no choice but to have good relations with them

③ 그들의 전반적인 수익이 성장했다는 것은 사실입니다   it is true that their overall revenue has increased

3 당신의 의견에 동의하지 않는 것은 아니지만, ~.

I don't mean to disagree with you, but ....

① 우리는 회사의 규모를 줄일 필요가 있습니다   we need to downsize our company

② 우리의 주가가 계속해서 떨어질 수 있습니다   our stock price could continue to drop

③ 회사 식당을 보수하는 것이 좋겠습니다   our company cafeteria should be renovated

4 ~하는 것을 제안 드리고 싶습니다.

I would like to propose that ....

① 진행 상황을 점검하기 위해 간단한 전화 회의를 여는   we have a brief phone meeting to follow up on the progress

② 전국적으로 태양열 철도 시스템 건설하는   we build a nationwide solar-powered rail system

③ 당신의 투자 계획을 재고하는   you reconsider your investment plan

Writing Exercise

A Complete the sentences using the given words.

1 이곳의 안 좋은 기상 상황 때문에, 우리는 회의를 7월 말로 미루었습니다.
(due to / move back)

▶ _____.

2 그가 저에게 일찍 가서 회의를 위한 모든 것을 준비하라고 지시했습니다.
(order / go in early / prepare)

▶ _____.

3 그 직원들을 해고해야 한다는 당신의 말에 진심으로 동의합니다.
(wholeheartedly / agree with you)

▶ _____.

4 프로젝트가 끝날 때까지 직원들이 열심히 일하도록 격려함으로써 저의 몫을 다하겠습니다.
(do one's part / encourage / complete)

▶ _____.

5 그들의 요청을 거절하겠다는 당신의 결정에 전적으로 동의합니다.
(be in agreement with / decision / reject)

▶ _____.

6 당신 말에 동의하지만, 가장 중요한 것은 이 절망적인 상황에서 탈출할 방법을 찾는 것입니다.
(tend to / what matters most / escape from)

▶ _____.

7 당신의 의견에 반대하려는 것은 아니지만, 우선 우리의 인트라넷 시스템에 무슨 일이 발생했는지 알아내야 할 것 같습니다.
(mean to / what is happening with)

▶ _____.

8 이 음반의 무료 MP3 파일 다운로드 제공을 고려해볼 것을 제안합니다.
(propose / consider / offer / these recordings)

▶ _____.

Refer to the Korean and complete the emails.

1 워크숍을 개최해주셔서 감사 드립니다, 헨리 월든 씨. 워크숍에서 당신이 제안한 것에 대한 저의 의견을 알려 드리겠습니다. 대책 위원회를 구성해야 할 것이라는 당신의 의견에 동의합니다. 사실, 이미 거기에 합류할 마케터 세 명을 뽑아놓았습니다. 그 세 사람의 이름과 직책이 들어 있는 명단을 첨부합니다.

_____, Mr. Henry Waldon. I would like to let you know my opinion on the proposal that you made at the workshop. _____ _____. In fact, I have already selected three marketers to join it. Please find attached a list of _____.

2 6개월에 한 번씩 직원을 재배치해야 한다는 당신의 의견에 감사 드립니다. 당신의 의견에 반대하려는 것은 아니지만 너무 자주라는 생각이 들고, 2년에 한 번 해야 한다고 생각합니다.

_____ that we need to relocate the workers once every six months. _____ I think it is too often and should occur once every two years.

3 현재의 가격대를 고려할 때 녹음 기능을 B&B 플레이어에 추가하는 것은 쉽지 않다고 생각합니다. 대신에 B&B 플레이어 2세대에 그것을 추가하는 것을 제안하고 싶습니다.

_____ to the B&B player considering the current price range. Instead, _____ to the second generation B&B player.

+ **TRY!** 자유롭게 나만의 이메일을 써보세요.

마케팅 부서에서 현재 내년도 마케팅 계획(marketing plan)을 짜고 있는데, 그 일환으로 내년에는 새롭게 TV광고(TV commercial)를 시도해보겠다며, 이에 대해 어떻게 생각하는지 묻는 메일을 당신에게 보내왔다. 각 부서의 예산 편성권을 갖고 있는 재무부장(financial director)으로서, 당신이 그들의 아이디어에 동의하거나 반대하는 간단한 이유를 들며 답장을 쓰고자 한다.

■ 정답은 없습니다.

문제점에 대해 논의하기

Talking about Problems

Subject	MusicPhone Development
From	HD@mphone.com
To	mylene@mphone.com

67.mp3

Mylene,

You told us that the development of the MusicPhone would be done by late June. However, I never heard the news that it is finished. It's already August, which is way past June.

Our dealers in the States are eagerly waiting for the MusicPhone since they have already started advertising it.

Please keep in mind that any further delay in its development will cause us financial hardship.

Once again, I would like to ask you to set a firm development schedule and to let us know it by the end of the week.

Hae-dong Oh
Marketing Manager

제목: 뮤직폰 개발
마일린

뮤직폰 개발이 6월 말에 완료될 것이라고 당신이 말했었죠. 하지만 끝났다는 소식을 듣지 못했습니다. 벌써 6월이 훨씬 지난 8월입니다.

미국에 있는 딜러들이 뮤직폰을 애타게 기다리고 있습니다. 벌써 광고를 시작했거든요.

더 이상 개발이 지연되면 우리에게 재정적인 압박이 있을 것이라는 점을 명심하세요.

다시 한 번 확실한 개발 일정을 잡아서 이번 주말까지 우리에게 알려주길 요청합니다.

오해동
마케팅 부장

be done 끝나다, 완료되다 _ be finished와 같은 뜻

Work under the current contract will **be done** by the end of next year.
▶ 현재 계약되어 있는 업무는 내년 말에 끝날 것입니다.

다른 의미 **be done**은 '행해지다' 또는 '수행되다'의 의미로도 쓰인다.

The meeting will **be done** according to the following schedule.
▶ 다음과 같은 일정으로 회의가 행해질 겁니다.

I never heard the news that ~라는 소식을 듣지 못했습니다

I never heard the news that you were selected as a new vice president.
▶ 당신이 새 부사장으로 선출되었다는 소식을 듣지 못했어요.

유사 표현 **It is news to me that** ~은 처음 듣는 말인데요

It is news to me that our engineers don't take this project seriously.
▶ 우리 엔지니어들이 이 프로젝트를 진지하게 여기지 않는다는 것은 처음 듣는 말인데요.

We are eagerly waiting for ~을 애타게 기다리고 있습니다

We are eagerly waiting for him to return from his vacation.
▶ 우리는 그가 휴가에서 복귀하기를 애타게 기다리고 있어요.

Please keep in mind that ~을 명심하세요

Please keep in mind that you are not allowed to remove any of the furniture in the office.
▶ 사무실의 어떠한 가구도 없애서는 안 된다는 것을 명심하세요.

유사 표현 **Be careful not to** ~하지 않도록 주의하세요.

Be careful not to smoke during working hours.
▶ 업무 시간에 담배를 피지 않도록 주의하세요.

Fill in the blanks with the appropriate expressions.

1 당신의 귀중한 의견을 애타게 기다리고 있습니다.

▶ We are _____ _____ _____ you to provide your valuable feedback.

2 품질 보증 검토는 필요한 기술을 갖춘 프로그래머에 의해 행해질 것입니다.

▶ Quality assurance reviews _____ _____ _____ by a programmer with the required skills.

3 누스 박사가 곧 은퇴할 것이라는 소식을 전혀 듣지 못했습니다.

▶ I _____ _____ _____ _____ that Dr. Nuss is retiring soon.

4 소심하게 행동하지 말아야 한다는 것을 명심하세요.

▶ _____ _____ _____ _____ that you need to stop being so timid.

5 고위 경영진으로부터 너무 많은 관심을 얻지 않도록 주의하세요.

▶ Be _____ _____ _____ get too much attention from top management.

Actual Sample

1 "엄중히 경고합니다" [문제가 발생하여 경고할 때]

▶ 향후 같은 문제가 다시 발생하지 않도록 문제를 일으킨 사람에게 다음과 같은 경고성 메시지를 작성할 수도 있다.

> **Let this serve as a fair warning**: If you continue to bad-mouth your boss and co-workers, you will be suspended for a month.

엄중히 경고합니다: 계속해서 당신 상사와 동료들을 험담하면 한 달 동안 직무 정지를 받게 될 것입니다.

2 "~을 알고 매우 실망했습니다" [실망을 나타낼 때]

▶ 문제 발생 시 바로 문제점을 짚기보다는 당신이 얼마나 당혹감을 느끼는지 알릴 때 쓸 수 있는 표현이다.

> **We are very disappointed to learn that** you promoted Jenna to sales director ahead of Sean.

당신이 션보다도 지나를 먼저 영업이사로 승진시켰다는 것을 알고 매우 실망했습니다.

3 "~에 대한 사과를 받아주세요" [문제의 책임을 시인할 때]

▶ 문제를 심각성을 최소화하는 방법은 일단 사과부터 하고 보는 것이다.

> **Please accept our apology for** the delay in scheduling the training program, and we hope that it did not cause any serious inconvenience.

훈련 프로그램의 일정을 잡는 데 생긴 지연에 대한 사과를 받아주십시오. 그리고 이것이 심각한 불편을 끼치지 않았기를 바랍니다.

4 "어려움은 ~에 있습니다" [문제 발생 원인을 말할 때]

▶ 문제 발생에 대한 근본 원인을 나타내는 표현이다.

> **The difficulty lies in** locating the virus in our network system. We are doing our best to get the system back to work. However, we believe it will take at least two weeks to get the job done.

우리 네트워크 시스템에서 바이러스의 위치를 찾는 데 어려움이 있습니다. 다시 시스템이 작동하도록 최선을 다하고 있습니다. 하지만 작업이 다 끝나려면 적어도 2주는 걸릴 것으로 보입니다.

Pattern Training

1 엄중히 경고합니다: ~.
Let this serve as a fair warning: _____.

① 제 주문품이 이틀 이내에 여기 도착해야 합니다   My order must arrive here within two days

② 당신은 즉시 정정 조치를 취해야 합니다   You must take corrective actions immediately

③ 제안서 제출 마감일에 변경은 없습니다   There is no change in the deadline for submitting a proposal

2 ~을 알고 매우 실망했습니다.
We are very disappointed to learn that _____.

① 당신이 계약을 따내지 못했다는 것   you failed to win the contract

② 그것이 기능상의 많은 문제를 가지고 있다는 것   it has a lot of functional problems

③ 아직 내 주문품을 보내지 않았다는 것   you haven't sent my order yet

3 ~에 대한 사과를 받아주세요.
Please accept our apology for _____.

① 우리가 초래한 불편함   the inconvenience we have caused

② 워크숍 취소   the cancellation of the workshop

③ 회의에 참석 못한 것   not showing up for the meeting

4 어려움은 ~에 있습니다.
The difficulty lies in _____.

① 향수병을 디자인하는 데   designing a perfume bottle

② 우리 조직에서 효율적인 팀워크를 발달시키는 데   developing effective teamwork in our own organization

③ 그 계획을 실행할 시기를 결정하는 데   deciding when to execute the plan

Writing Exercise

A Complete the sentences using the given words.

1 그 거래가 성사된 후에 우리 주가가 떨어졌습니다.
(stock / fall / be done)

▶ _____.

2 당신이 건강 상태 때문에 회사를 떠난다는 소식을 들었어요.
(hear the news / leave / because of)

▶ _____.

3 우리는 더 낮은 가격의 새로운 모델을 애타게 기다리고 있습니다.
(wait for / lower price)

▶ _____.

4 당신의 업무 스타일에 대해 우려하는 목소리가 있다는 것을 명심하세요.
(keep in mind / some concerns / working style)

▶ _____.

5 엄중히 경고합니다: 우리의 규정을 어기는 것을 참지 않을 것입니다.
(a fair warning / put up with / violate)

▶ _____.

6 당신이 워크숍에 참가하지 않으려 한다는 걸 알고 우리는 매우 실망했습니다.
(disappointed / intend to / participate in)

▶ _____.

7 귀사의 웹사이트에서 일어난 기술적인 결함에 대한 저희의 진심 어린 사과를 받아주십시오.
(sincerest apology / technical glitches / happen)

▶ _____.

8 어려움은 이 문제에 대한 올바른 해결책을 찾는 데 있습니다.
(lie in / find / right solution)

▶ _____.

B Refer to the Korean and complete the emails.

1 내년도 생산 일정 회의에 참석할 수 없다는 걸 알고 매우 실망했습니다. 당신 없이는 어떠한 확실한 결정도 내릴 수 없습니다. 회의를 위해서 일정을 비워주세요.

> _____ you won't be able to make it to the meeting on next year's production schedule. _____ without you. Please clear your schedule for the meeting.

2 엄중히 경고합니다: 우리의 단골 고객들을 대하는 데 당신이 잘못했다는 것을 인정할 마지막 기회입니다. 그들은 지금 우리 회사를 상대로 법적 대응을 고려하고 있습니다.

> _____ : _____ admit you made a mistake in dealing with our loyal customers. They are considering _____ _____.

3 우선, 오해가 있었던 점에 사과 드립니다. 어려움은 우리가 다른 시간대에서 일하고 있다는 사실에 있습니다. 그래서 제때 귀하의 이메일에 답변을 드리지 못했습니다.

> First of all, _____. _____ _____ with different time zones. So we haven't been able to reply to your emails in time.

+ TRY! 자유롭게 이메일을 써보세요.

> 당신은 지난주에 제품 로드맵(product roadmap)을 5월 20일까지 보내달라고 상품 기획팀(product planning team)에 두 번(twice)이나 요청했는데, 아직까지도 답변을 받지 못했다. 이메일을 통해 실망감을 표시하고 내일까지 제품 로드맵을 보내달라고 요구하려 한다.

■ 정답은 없습니다.

도움이나 조언 요청하기

Asking for Help or Advice

Subject	Help Needed
From	michelle@coffeebug.com
To	BR@coffeebug.com

68.mp3

Mr. Bob Reid,

As you know, we are preparing for a presentation on our product roadmap for 2020.

I hate to trouble you, but we are in need of a person with superb PowerPoint skills, including using multimedia objects and custom animations, adding interactions, and publishing completed presentations.

I was informed that there is a person named Robert Horry in your department who is good at PowerPoint. It would be greatly helpful if we could work with him for a week.

Many thanks,
Michelle Presson
Task Force Team Leader

제목: 도움 요청

밥 라이드 부장님께,

아시다시피 저희는 2020년 제품 로드맵에 대한 발표를 준비하고 있습니다.

귀찮게 해드리고 싶진 않지만, 멀티미디어 프로그램과 맞춤식 애니메이션을 이용하고 상호작용 프로그램을 넣어 발표 자료를 완성할 수 있는 훌륭한 파워포인트 기술을 가진 사람이 필요합니다.

부장님 부서에 로버트 호리라고 파워포인트에 능숙한 사람이 있다고 들어 알고 있습니다. 일주일 동안 그 사람과 함께 일할 수 있다면 아주 큰 도움이 될 것 같습니다.

감사합니다.
미셸 프레슨
TF팀 팀장

prepare for ~을 준비하다

We are **preparing for** our Christmas event on December 24.
▶ 저희는 12월 24일에 있을 크리스마스 행사를 준비하고 있습니다.

유사표현 **get ready for** ~을 위해 준비하다
Get ready for the next generation of the sea-changing mobile phone.
▶ 그 혁신적인 휴대전화의 다음 세대를 위해 준비하세요.

I hate to trouble you, but 귀찮게 해드리고 싶진 않지만 _ 도움을 청하는 정중한 표현

I hate to trouble you, but I have changed the name and URL of my homepage.
▶ 귀찮게 해드리고 싶진 않지만 제 홈페이지 이름과 URL을 변경했습니다.

유사표현 **I don't want to bother you, but** 성가시게 해드리고 싶진 않지만 ~

I was informed that ~라고 들어 알고 있습니다 _ 누군가에게 정보를 들어 that 이하의 내용을 알고 있다는 의미다.

I was informed that you have a tendency to always try to do things perfectly.
▶ 당신은 매사를 완벽하게 하려는 경향이 있다고 들어 알고 있습니다.

유사표현 **I was told that** ~라고 들어서 알고 있습니다

be good at ~에 능숙하다 _ 어떠한 일에 숙련된 기술을 가지고 있을 때 쓸 수 있는 표현

I am good at identifying areas that need improvement.
▶ 저는 개선이 필요한 분야를 찾아내는 데 능숙합니다.

It would be greatly helpful if ~한다면 큰 도움이 될 것입니다

It would be greatly helpful if you answer these questions.
▶ 이 질문들에 답변해주시면 많은 도움이 될 것입니다.

유사표현 **I would really appreciate it if** ~한다면 정말 감사하겠습니다.

Vocabulary Check-Up

Fill in the blanks with the appropriate expressions.

1 귀찮게 해드리고 싶진 않지만 그저 당신의 확인을 받고 싶을 뿐입니다.
▶ I _____ to _____ _____, but I just want to get your confirmation.

2 미리 회의를 준비해야 합니다.
▶ We _____ _____ _____ the meeting in advance.

3 그 행사를 위해 적절하게 차려 입어야 한다고 들어 알고 있습니다.
▶ _____ _____ _____ that we would have to dress professionally for the ceremony.

4 그는 파워포인트를 사용하는 데 능숙하지 않습니다.
▶ He is _____ _____ _____ using PowerPoint.

5 이 소프트웨어를 제 기기에 어떻게 설치하는지 구체적으로 조언해주실 수 있다면 큰 도움이 되겠습니다.
▶ It would be _____ _____ if you could specifically _____ me how I can install this software on my device.

Actual Sample

1 "~ 좀 해주세요" [도움을 완곡하게 요청할 때]

> **I would like you to** participate in the discussion: Question the presenters, and bring out what you see as important points that have been neglected.

당신이 토론에 참여해주시기를 바랍니다. 발표자에게 질문하고, 등한시되고 있는 중요한 점들을 제기해주세요.

2 "~에 대해 조언 좀 해주세요" [조언을 구하고자 할 때]

> **I would like to ask your advice on** how to find a reliable website architect and developer. My business venture requires an interactive website with user profiles, a message board, and an internal email system.

믿을 만한 웹사이트 설계자와 개발자를 찾는 방법에 대해 당신의 조언을 구합니다. 제 벤처 사업은 사용자 프로필, 게시판, 그리고 내부 이메일 시스템을 갖춘 양방향 웹사이트가 필요합니다.

3 "~하기를 조언 드립니다" [상대방에게 조언할 때]

> If you plan a new project in your organization, **I advise you to** read the excellent article in the attached magazine and review the comments made by Seth Godin.

귀하의 조직에서 새로운 프로젝트를 구상하고 있다면, 첨부해드린 잡지에 있는 훌륭한 기사를 읽어보시고 세스 고딘의 코멘트를 참고하시기를 조언 드립니다.

4 "당신의 조언을 받아들일게요" [조언을 받아들이겠다는 의사를 표현할 때]

> **We decided to take your advice** and will no longer do business with or invest in companies that dodge taxes.

당신의 조언을 받아들이기로 결정했고, 더 이상 세금을 회피하는 회사들과 사업을 하거나 투자하지 않을 것입니다.

Pattern Training

1 당신이 ~해주셨으면 합니다.
I would like you to _____.

① 저희 웹사이트의 메인 페이지를 업데이트해   update the main page of our website

② 가능한 한 빨리 서버를 교체해   replace the server ASAP

③ 걱정거리가 있을 경우 우리와 상의해   consult us in the event that you have any concerns

2 ~에 대해 당신의 조언을 구하고자 합니다.
I would like to ask your advice on _____.

① 항공 관련 직업에 대해   a career in aviation

② 우리 디지털 카메라에 사용될 배터리에 대해   batteries for use in our digital cameras

③ 그들이 제 편지에 답장을 거부했기 때문에 이를 어떻게 처리해야 하는지에 대해   how to handle this since they refuse to reply to my letters

3 ~하기를 조언 드립니다.
I advise you to _____.

① 웹사이트 연결 속도를 점검하시기를   check the website connection speed

② 그 멀티미디어 플레이어에 대해 설문조사를 실시하시기를   conduct a survey on the multimedia player

③ 그들의 주문품을 항공 화물로 보내시기를   ship their order by air freight

4 당신의 조언을 받아들이기로 결정했고 ~.
We decided to take your advice and _____.

① 그 컨설턴트와 계속 연락할 것입니다   will keep in touch with the consultant

② 그 불량 식기세척기를 교체할 것입니다   will replace the defective dishwasher

③ 그 프로젝트를 일시 중단할 것입니다   will put a temporary freeze on the project

Writing Exercise

A   Complete the sentences using the given words.

1   저희는 미시건 주립 대학교에서 개최되는 곧 있을 워크숍을 준비하고 있습니다.
(prepare for / hold)

▶ _____.

2   당신을 귀찮게 해드리고 싶진 않지만 도움을 요청하고 싶습니다.
(bother / ask for)

▶ _____.

3   이메일 보내는 방법을 가르쳐주시면 정말 고맙겠습니다.
(appreciate / instruct / send)

▶ _____.

4   당신이 여행업계에 대해 박식하다고 들어 알고 있습니다.
(be informed / knowledgeable / travel industry)

▶ _____.

5   이 문제와 관련해 누구에게 물어야 하는지 저에게 알려주시면 정말 고맙겠습니다.
(greatly helpful / regarding this matter)

▶ _____.

6   이 프로그램을 더 잘 사용하는 방법을 저에게 알려주셨으면 합니다.
(would like / how to / better use)

▶ _____.

7   미리 티켓을 예약하는 방법에 대해 조언해주셨으면 합니다.
(ask one's advice / how to book)

▶ _____.

8   보고서를 제때 끝내기 위해 그와 함께 일할 것을 조언 드립니다.
(advise / work with / on time)

▶ _____.

Refer to the Korean and complete the emails.

1 이미 GH Navigator 3가 설치되어 있는 제 기기에서 내비게이션 시스템을 사용할 수 있는 방법을 구체적으로 조언해주시면 큰 도움이 되겠습니다.

> _____ how I can use
> the navigation system on my device when the GH Navigator 3 software is already installed.

2 답장 속도와 보내주신 정보에 매우 감명을 받았습니다. 그리고 아시다시피 저희는 당신의 조언을 받아들이기로 결정했고 그 은행 계좌를 닫았습니다.

> _____ both the speed of the reply and the information given.
> And, as you know, _____.

3 제 말에 좀 더 귀 기울여주시고, 그 문제에 대해 마음을 열어주셨으면 합니다. 즉, 그 문제를 심각하게 받아들여야 합니다. 그 불량품들을 당장 재작업해주실 것을 다시 한 번 요청 드립니다.

> _____ and have an open mind about this issue.
> In other words, _____. I ask you one more time to rework
> the defective units right away.

+ TRY! 자유롭게 이메일을 써보세요.

> 당신은 현재 상품기획 팀(product planning team) 팀장이다. 스페인 시장에 출시할 새로운 식품을 개발하려 하는데, 소비자들이 어떤 것을 원하는지(customers' needs) 알 필요가 있다. 그래서 해외 마케팅 팀(overseas marketing team) 팀장 Mr.Cha에게 스페인 소비자들의 취향(what they like)에 대해 조언을 얻고자 한다.

■ 정답은 없습니다.

Answers &
Audio Scripts

Vocabulary Check-up p.13

A 1 ⓒ 2 ⓐ 3 ⓔ 4 ⓓ 5 ⓑ

B 1 arrange 2 purpose / discuss 3 table 4 last
5 attend / on

C 1 coffee break 2 What / want 3 attend / urgent
4 items / discuss 5 meeting agenda

Conversation 1 회의 소집하기 p.14   01.mp3

A: 회의를 소집해야겠습니다.

B: 회의의 목적이 무엇인데요, 토마스?

A: 다음 달 생산 일정에 대해 얘기해볼 필요가 있어요. 수요일에 회의할 수 있
겠어요?

B: 죄송하지만 수요일은 어려울 것 같아요. 고객을 만나기로 되어 있거든요.
목요일 오전은 어때요?

A: 목요일 오전은 좋아요. 그럼 10시에 401호실에서 모입시다.

B: 알겠습니다. 저희 팀원들에게 공지해두겠습니다. 그때 뵙죠.

Conversation 2 안건 소개하기 p.15   02.mp3

A: 여러분 모두 와주셔서 정말 고맙습니다. 오늘 회의 의제로 다룰 사항이 두
가지 있습니다. 하나는 이달의 직원을 뽑는 것이고, 다른 하나는 엔지니어
인력을 더 고용하는 것입니다.

B: 의제에 하나 더 추가할 수 있을까요?

A: 물론이죠. 말씀해보세요

B: 조립 라인을 좀 더 추가하는 것에 대해 얘기하고 싶습니다.

A: 안 될 이유가 없죠. 회의 후반부에 논의하겠습니다.

C: 회의가 얼마나 걸릴까요?

A: 두 시간 정도 걸릴 거예요. 그리고 두 번째 안건을 진행하기 전에 10분간
휴식을 가질 겁니다.

Practice 1 Let's Speak p.16

A 1 minutes 2 agenda / add 3 looks / difficult 4 cover

B 1 I want to arrange a meeting. /
When would be a good time to get together?
2 What's the purpose of the meeting? / So we are here to
discuss how to process the orders more quickly.

Practice 2 Listen-up p.17

Audio Script − A, B   03.mp3

Sophia Thank you for coming after working hours. I've
asked you here because I'd like to discuss several
changes to our company policy.

Donald What time do you think the meeting will end?

Sophia It depends on how well we understand each
other's position.

Donald Okay.

Sophia The first agenda item is the sick leave policy, and
the second one is the overtime work policy. We
will take a 5-minute break after discussing the first
one.

소피아 근무 시간 후에 와주셔서 고맙습니다. 우리 회사 정책에서 몇 가지 변경 사
항에 대해 논의해보고자 모여달라고 했습니다.

도널드 회의가 언제 끝날 것 같요?

소피아 서로의 입장을 얼마나 잘 이해하느냐에 달려 있죠.

도널드 알겠습니다.

소피아 첫 번째 안건은 병가 규정이고, 두 번째는 초과근무에 대한 규정입니다. 첫
번째 안건을 논의한 후에 5분간 휴식을 가질 겁니다.

A 1 To discuss several changes to their company policies.
2 It depends on how well they understand each other's
position.
3 Two.
4 After discussing the first agenda item.

B 1 after working hours 2 I'd like to discuss
3 the meeting will end 4 It depends on
5 The first agenda item 6 take a 5-minute break

Audio Script − C   04.mp3

A Dan, did you check your email?

B Not yet. Why?

A Alex called a meeting.

B Really? What's that for?

A He wants to exchange some ideas about our product
designs.

B I see. When is the meeting?

A It's tomorrow afternoon at 3 in Meeting Room 16.

A 댄, 이메일 체크했어요?

B 아직이요. 왜요?

A 알렉스가 회의를 소집했어요.

B 정말요? 무엇 때문이죠?

A 우리 제품의 디자인에 관해서 의견을 좀 나누고 싶어해요.

B 그렇군요. 회의가 언제죠?

A 16번 회의실에서 내일 오후 3시에요.

C 1 True 2 True 3 False 4 False

WEEK 02 \ 안건 토의하기

Vocabulary Check-up p.19

A 1 ⓑ 2 ⓓ 3 ⓐ 4 ⓒ 5 ⓔ

B 1 wrong / concern 2 Why 3 obvious
4 my opinion 5 what / saying

C 1 your opinion[view] 2 seems / need
3 as / concerned 4 think / produce
5 any suggestions

Conversation 1 안건에 대해 의견 묻기 p.20 05.mp3

A: 첫 번째 안건부터 시작합시다. 원가 절감에 관한 것인데요. 새미, 당신이 이 문제에 대한 보고서를 준비한 것으로 알고 있습니다.

B: 네, 맞습니다.

A: 시작하시죠.

B: 네, 제가 조사한 바에 따르면, 우리는 보안과 같은 간접비용에 너무 많은 돈을 쓰고 있습니다.

A: 그러면 간접비용을 줄이는 데 도움이 될 만한 제안사항이라도 있나요?

B: 물론입니다. 현재의 보안 시스템을 바꿔야 한다고 생각해요. 현재의 보안 시스템은 유지하는 데 돈이 많이 듭니다.

A: 그렇군요. 그 점에 대해 수잔의 의견을 들어볼 수 있을까요?

Conversation 2 의견 피력하기 p.21 06.mp3

A: 제 생각에는, 초과근무 체계를 조정할 필요가 있어요.

B: 무슨 얘기죠?

A: 현재 전원이 매일 초과근무 시간을 이메일로 인사부로 보내고 있습니다.

B: 그게 뭐가 문제죠?

A: 이는 인사과 직원들이 정보 처리하는 것을 너무 어렵게 만들고 있어요.

B: 그래서 제안사항이 뭐가요?

A: 월 단위로 초과근무 시간을 보내는 것을 제안합니다. 그런 방식이면, 실수 없이 정보를 처리할 여유가 생길 겁니다.

B: 좋은 생각인 것 같네요.

Practice 1 Let's Speak p.22

A 1 It seems to me there is room for cooperation between the two firms.
2 It is obvious that our workers are superior to other workers.
3 My point is that nobody wants to take over his place.
4 I suggest that we offer an incentive program for the sales staff.

B 1 ⓑ 2 ⓐ, ⓓ 3 ⓒ

Practice 2 Listen-up p.23

Audio Script – A, B 07.mp3

Manager	Let's go on to the second item. It's about our bridge construction project. According to the weekly progress report, I found that it's still in its infancy. Did you know that? The deadline for the project is coming up in just two months.
Robert	In my opinion, we should hire more workers to complete it on time.
Manager	Do you have any suggestions that would help us find more engineers as soon as possible?
Robert	I recommend that we put a want ad in the local paper.
Manager	I think that's a good idea.

부장	두 번째 항목으로 넘어갑시다. 교량 건설 프로젝트에 관한 것인데요. 주간 진행 보고서에 따르면, 프로젝트가 여전히 초기 단계에 머물고 있는 게 보이네요. 그거 알아요? 프로젝트 마감일이 겨우 두 달 앞으로 다가왔어요.
로버트	제 생각에는, 제때 끝마치려면 더 많은 직원을 고용해야 합니다.
부장	가능한 한 빨리 기술자들을 더 고용하는 데 도움이 될 만한 제안사항이 있나요?
로버트	지역신문에 구인광고를 낼 것을 제안합니다.
부장	그거 좋은 생각인 것 같군요.

A 1 False 2 True 3 True

B 1 go on to 2 According to 3 coming up in
4 In my opinion 5 any suggestions 6 I recommend

Audio Script – C 08.mp3

Walker	Fiona, what's your opinion about this?
Fiona	Well, I think the gym in the company is outdated.
Walker	What do you mean?
Fiona	The space is too small, so it only accommodates 30 people at once.
Walker	So what's your suggestion?
Fiona	I'd like to have it renovated.
Walker	Hmm…. It would cost us a lot of money.
Fiona	Mr. Walker, I want you to think about our workers' health.

워커	피오나, 이에 대한 당신 의견은 어때요?
피오나	음, 저는 사내 체육관이 낡았다고 생각해요.
워커	무슨 얘기죠?
피오나	공간이 너무 좁아서 한 번에 겨우 30명만 수용하잖아요.
워커	그래서 제안하는 것이 뭐죠?
피오나	보수공사를 했으면 합니다.
워커	흠… 돈이 많이 들 텐데요.
피오나	워커 씨, 우리 직원들의 건강을 생각해주셨으면 합니다.

C 1 The gym in the company.
2 30 people.
3 It is too small.
4 Renovating the gym would cost a lot of money.

Vocabulary Check-up p.25

A 1 ⓑ 2 ⓓ 3 ⓔ 4 ⓐ 5 ⓒ

B 1 fruitful 2 interrupt 3 basically
4 decided 5 covered

C 1 action items 2 reached a conclusion
3 finish my point 4 return 5 summarize[recap]

Conversation 1 끼어들기 및 통제하기 p.26 09.mp3

A: 실례지만, 잠시 끼어들어도 될까요?
B: 물론이죠, 말씀하세요.
A: 우리의 시장점유율을 회복하기 위해서는 중국에 지점을 둬야 한다고 생각합니다.
B: 소피아, 논지에서 벗어나는 것 같군요. 그건 의제에 없는 내용이에요.
A: 죄송합니다. 하지만 제 요점을 마저 말씀 드릴게요.
B: 그건 다음 회의로 미루는 게 어때요?
A: 알겠습니다. 문제 없습니다.
B: 계속해서 세 번째 안건을 논의할까요?
C: 네, 직원들의 사기 진작을 위해 토요일은 쉬어야 한다고 생각합니다.
B: 오, 죄송하지만 시간이 얼마 없네요. 2분 안에 요점만 말씀해주실래요?

Conversation 2 요약하기 및 끝맺기 p.27 10.mp3

A: 올리비아, 우리가 합의한 사항을 요약해주실래요?
B: 그러죠. 기본적으로 우리는 그 제품을 계속해서 아웃소싱하는 것에 동의했습니다.
A: 회의 요약본을 이번 주말까지 우리에게 이메일로 보내줬으면 해요.
B: 그렇게 하죠.
A: 더 협의할 사항 있나요?
C: 아니요. 모든 문제들을 다룬 것 같습니다.
A: 좋습니다. 시간이 다 되었으니 여기서 끝냅시다. 오늘 아주 좋은 진전이 있었어요.
D: 다른 회의를 하기로 하지 않았나요?
A: 네, 회의 날짜 이틀 전에 모든 참석자들께 상기 메일을 보내겠습니다. 참석해주셔서 고맙습니다.

Practice 1 Let's Speak p.28

A 1 We made some good progress today.
2 You seem to be getting off the point.
3 We have decided to offer customers 10%-off coupons for August.
4 Can we go on to discuss the second issue?
5 Could you sum up the decisions we have made?
6 I'm very sorry to interrupt, but may I ask a question?

B 1 Please speak one by one.
2 Why don't we postpone the third issue until the next meeting?
3 To sum up the discussion, we will build a website to attract more customers.

4 I think we've finally reached a conclusion. / Thanks for your participation.

Practice 2 Listen-up p.29

Audio Script – A, B 11.mp3

Lisa	May I interrupt you for a moment?
Manager	Sure, go ahead.
Lisa	We should knock 50% off the prices of all items during the summer sale.
Manager	Lisa, you seem to be getting off the point. We're not talking about the prices but about the quality of our products.
Lisa	Oh, I'm sorry. But please let me finish my point.
Manager	Sorry, but we should just deal with the quality issue only.
Lisa	Okay.
Manager	Let's move on to the third agenda item.

리사	잠시만 제가 끼어들어도 될까요?
부장	물론이죠, 말씀하세요.
리사	여름 세일 기간 동안 전 품목을 50% 할인해야 합니다.
부장	리사, 논점에서 벗어난 것 같네요. 제품의 가격이 아니라 품질에 대해 논의하는 중입니다.
리사	아, 죄송합니다. 하지만 제 얘기를 끝내게 해주세요.
부장	미안하지만 품질 문제만 다룹시다.
리사	알겠습니다.
부장	세 번째 안건으로 넘어갑시다.

A 1 The quality of their products.
2 The summer sale.
3 Two.

B 1 May I interrupt 2 We should knock
3 getting off the point 4 finish my point
5 deal with the quality issue 6 Let's move on to

Audio Script – C 12.mp3

Manager	We are running out of time. Is there anything more to discuss?
Susan	No. I think we've covered all the issues that we were supposed to talk about today.
Manager	All right. Let's stop here then.
Allan	I think we've made very good progress today.
Manager	Right. Allan, could you send us a copy of the minutes so we can share it with our team members?
Allan	Sure thing.
Susan	I believe we need another meeting to discuss our sales plan.
Manager	You're right, Susan. But I've got to leave right now to attend a workshop. Why don't we set the meeting date and time tomorrow?

부장	시간이 없습니다. 더 논의할 게 있나요?
수잔	아니요. 오늘 이야기하기로 한 건 다 한 것 같습니다.
부장	좋습니다. 그러면 여기서 끝내죠.
앨런	오늘 아주 좋은 성과가 있었던 것 같아요.
부장	그래요. 앨런, 팀원들과 공유할 수 있게 회의 요약본을 우리에게 보내주실래요?
앨런	물론이죠.
수잔	매출 계획을 논의하기 위해 또 한 번 회의를 할 필요가 있을 것 같습니다.
부장	맞습니다, 수잔. 그런데 저는 워크숍에 참석해야 해서 지금 당장 자리를 떠야 합니다. 회의 날짜와 시간은 내일 정하는 게 어떨까요?

C 1 True 2 True 3 False 4 False

PLUS WEEK \ 동의하기 및 반대하기

Vocabulary Check-up p.31

A 1 ⓑ 2 ⓔ 3 ⓐ 4 ⓒ 5 ⓓ

B 1 agree with 2 point out 3 against 4 My meaning
5 emphasize

C 1 see what 2 In other 3 disagree 4 What / do
5 To make / short

Conversation 1 동의하기 및 반대하기 p.32 13.mp3

A: 지난 5년간 미국에서 우리 매출이 떨어지고 있어요. 그래서 마케팅 전략을 수정하는 수밖에 없겠어요.
B: 거기에 일부 동의합니다만, 시장 크기가 줄어들었다는 것도 염두에 둬야죠.
A: 유감스럽지만 전 그렇게 생각하지 않습니다. 데이터리서치가 공개한 데이터를 봐주세요. 여전히 증가하고 있잖아요.
B: 정말이에요?
A: 네, 2016년 이후로 30% 증가했어요.
B: 줄어들고 있다고 생각했는데, 제가 틀렸네요. 정보 고마워요.
A: 상황을 반전시키기 위해선 무언가를 해야 합니다.

Conversation 2 의견 강조하기 p.33 14.mp3

A: 경쟁사들은 더 작은 제품들을 생산하고 있다는 것을 지적하고 싶습니다.
B: 맞아요. 그게 요즘 추세인 것 같아요.
A: KDT사가 새로운 제품을 출시했는데, 이전 모델보다 작은 것입니다.
B: 시장에서는 어떤가요?
A: 지금까지는 호평을 받고 있어요.
B: 현재의 추세를 따라가는 수밖에 없겠네요. 어떻게 생각해요?
A: 시장에 나와 있는 다른 제품과 차별화할 필요가 있다고 생각합니다.
B: 좀 더 자세히 말해봐요.
A: 간단히 말씀 드리면, 우리 제품을 작게 만들기보다는 크게 만드는 것이죠. 그게 우리가 생존할 수 있는 길이라고 믿습니다.

Practice 1 Let's Speak p.34

A 1 ⓐ 2 ⓓ 3 ⓒ 4 ⓔ 5 ⓑ

B 1 That's the way we can compete against our competitors.
2 In other words, we should consider what our company looks like from the outside.
3 I'm afraid that I don't think so.
4 Keep in mind that we can't control how our customers react.
5 I partly agree to that, but we can't change our plan.
6 I'd like to point out that we need to have a face-to-face meeting with them.

Practice 2 Listen-up p.35

Audio Script - A, B 15.mp3

Emily	Peter, in my opinion, we should switch CPU vendors.
Peter	Why is that?
Emily	Because our current vendor is charging us too much.
Peter	I see what you're saying, Emily. But money is not everything.
Emily	I'd like to point out that we can lower our product prices if we use other CPUs.
Peter	I'm not comfortable with your idea. Please keep in mind that they are second to none when it comes to product quality.
Emily	I know their CPUs are reliable, Peter. However, if we keep using their CPUs, we will lose our market share.

에밀리	피터, 제 생각엔 CPU 공급업체를 바꿔야 할 것 같아요.
피터	왜요?
에밀리	현재의 공급업체는 가격이 너무 비싸요.
피터	무슨 말인지 알겠어요, 에밀리. 하지만 돈이 다는 아니잖아요.
에밀리	다른 CPU를 사용하면 우리 제품 가격을 낮출 수 있다는 점을 지적하고 싶습니다.
피터	전 동의할 수가 없네요. 품질에 관한 한 그들이 최고라는 것을 명심하세요.
에밀리	그들의 CPU가 믿을 만하다는 것은 알아요, 피터. 하지만 그들의 CPU를 계속 사용한다면 우리는 시장점유율을 잃게 될 겁니다.

A 1 Switching CPU vendors.
2 They are charging too much.
3 Their product quality.
4 Losing their market share.

B 1 in my opinion 2 Why is that
3 see what you're saying 4 not comfortable with
5 keep in mind 6 lose our market share

Richard Sarah, I'd like to point out that AIZ is dominating the market now.

Sarah You can say that again. Their new album became a massive hit.

Richard We need to come up with a totally new marketing strategy.

Sarah What does that have to do with a marketing strategy, Richard?

Richard They spent a pretty penny advertising the album, and it's finally paying off.

Sarah But as you know, Richard, we're on a tight budget.

Richard We have no choice but to increase the budget for advertising.

Sarah Okay, Richard. I fully understand what you're saying. I'll discuss what you said with the rest of my team after the meeting and let you know what we decide.

리처드 사라, AIZ가 현재 시장을 장악하고 있다는 점을 지적하고 싶군요.

사라 맞는 말이에요. 그들의 새로운 앨범이 크게 히트했더군요.

리처드 우린 완전히 새로운 마케팅 전략을 세워야 해요.

사라 그게 마케팅 전략이랑 무슨 관계죠, 리처드?

리처드 그들은 앨범을 광고하는 데 엄청나게 많은 돈을 썼고, 마침내 효과를 보고 있어요.

사라 하지만 리처드, 알다시피 우리는 예산이 빠듯하잖아요.

리처드 광고 예산을 늘리는 수밖에 없죠.

사라 좋습니다, 리처드. 무슨 말인지 충분히 알겠습니다. 회의 후에 나머지 팀원들과 당신이 말했던 것을 의논하고 결정사항을 알려드릴게요.

C 1 True 2 False 3 False 4 True

PART 2 \ 비즈니스 프레젠테이션
Business Presentations

WEEK 04 \ 발표 목적과 발표자 소개

Vocabulary Check-up p.41

A 1 ⓑ 2 ⓐ 3 ⓓ 4 ⓔ 5 ⓒ

B 1 talk about 2 examine 3 is divided 4 Finally
5 After that

C 1 outline 2 take a look 3 Sales Department
4 ask / during 5 purpose[objective]

Presentation 1 발표자 소개하기 p.42   17.mp3

바쁘신데도 불구하고 시간을 내 저희와 함께해주셔서 감사합니다.
하워드 차 씨를 소개하고자 여러분들을 이 자리로 모셨습니다. 하워드 씨는 우리의 신임 프로젝트 컨설턴트로 고용되었습니다.
그는 이 분야에서 23년 이상의 경험이 있습니다. 지난 10년간 그는 쓰리스타 라고 하는 회사에서 일했습니다. 하워드 씨는 프로젝트 관리 전문가 협회 회원이며 필라델피아에 있는 드렉셀 대학교에서 박사학위를 받았습니다.
이제 그가 프로젝트를 효율적으로 운영하는 방법에 대해서 말하고자 합니다.
하워드 차 씨에게 큰 박수갈채 부탁 드립니다.

Presentation 2 발표 절차 안내하기 p.43   18.mp3

안녕하세요, 여러분.
여러분 모두 아시다시피 우리는 인도에서 시장 점유율을 잃고 있습니다. 이에 대해 수수방관만 하고 있을 수는 없죠. 저의 목표는 2년 내에 시장 점유율을 10~20퍼센트 올리는 것입니다. 작아지는 시장에서 어떻게 시장 점유율을 올릴 수 있을까요? 오늘 제 발표의 주제는 어떻게 이것을 할 수 있는가 하는 것입니다.
발표는 세 가지 주요 부문으로 나뉩니다. 우선, 현재의 시장 상황을 살펴볼 것입니다. 그리고 나서 여러분들께 우리의 제품들에 대해, 그리고 그것들이 어떻게 시장에 적합한지를 말씀드릴 것입니다. 끝으로 광고 전략을 몇 가지 자세히 살펴볼 것입니다.
발표는 30분 정도 걸릴 것입니다. 발표 후에 질문을 해주시면 감사하겠습니다.

Practice 1 Let's Speak p.44

A 1 Thank you for taking time off from your busy schedule to be with us.
2 I'm going to update you on the most important features of our brand-new product.
3 The purpose of my presentation is to discuss the company's policy on sick leave.
4 My presentation is divided into three sections.

5 My presentation will take around 20 minutes.

6 He has over 12 years of experience in this industry.

B 1 responsible 2 If / free 3 working / field

  4 take 5 as 6 subject

Practice 2 Listen-up p.45

Audio Script − A   19.mp3

Thank you all so much for coming to the Klein Awards
Ceremony. Let me introduce Dr. Klein first.
Dr. Klein established his own publishing company back in
1967. Since then, he has published over 10,000 children's
books. Also, he has a master's degree from Oklahoma
University.
And now he is going to talk about how to make useful
books for kids. Let's all give a warm welcome to Dr. Klein.

클라인 시상식에 와주셔서 감사합니다. 먼저 클라인 박사를 소개하겠습니다.
클라인 박사는 1967년에 자신의 출판사를 설립했습니다. 그 이후로 만 권이 넘는
아동 도서를 발간해왔습니다. 또한, 오클라호마 대학에서 석사 학위를 받았습니다.
그리고 이제 어떻게 하면 아이들에게 유용한 책을 만들 수 있을까에 대해 말씀하
시고자 합니다. 클라인 박사에게 따뜻한 환영의 박수를 주시기 바랍니다.

A 1 The publishing industry.

  2 Over 10,000.

  3 A master's degree.

  4 How to make useful books for kids.

Audio Script − B, C   20.mp3

Hello, folks! Thank you for being here. The subject of
my presentation this evening is how to score well on the
TOEIC.
My presentation is divided into three sections. Firstly,
I will tell you about how the TOEIC is constructed.
Secondly, I'm going to let you know how to prepare for
the exam in an efficient way. Finally, you will pick up
some useful problem-solving skills for the TOEIC test.
The presentation will take around 30 minutes. And there
will be a short break for refreshments before the Q&A
session.

안녕하세요, 여러분! 와주셔서 감사합니다. 오늘 밤 제 발표의 주제는 토익 점수를
잘 받는 방법에 관한 것입니다.
제 발표는 세 부분으로 나뉩니다. 우선, 토익이 어떻게 구성되어 있는지를 말씀 드
릴 것입니다. 둘째로, 효율적으로 시험을 준비하는 방법을 알려드릴 것입니다. 마
지막으로 토익 시험에 유용한 문제풀기 요령을 몇 가지 익히게 될 것입니다.
발표는 약 30분 정도 걸릴 것입니다. 그리고 질의응답 시간 전에 다과를 들 수 있게
짧은 휴식을 가질 것입니다.

B 1 False 2 True 3 False 4 False

C 1 for being here 2 The subject 3 divided into

  4 Firstly 5 let you know 6 Finally

  7 take around 30 8 a short break

WEEK 05 \ 발표 시작과 전개

Vocabulary Check-up p.47

A 1 ⓒ 2 ⓐ 3 ⓑ 4 ⓔ 5 ⓓ

B 1 turn to 2 pay attention 3 describe

  4 emphasize / too much 5 begin by

C 1 How many 2 Think / about 3 time / discuss

  4 come to know 5 with confidence

Presentation 1 발표 시작하기 p.48   21.mp3

우리의 해외 사업 철학에 관해서 몇 가지를 여러분과 공유하는 것으로 발표를
시작하겠습니다. 해외 사업의 철학은 혁신적인 제품을 소개한다는 장기적인
전략 투구에 기초하고 있습니다. 그것은 혁신 기술의 지속적인 이전입니다. 특
히 우리와 같은 기술 회사의 경우엔 거의 필수적이죠.
저의 주장을 뒷받침하기 위해 소니의 짧은 연혁으로 넘어가겠습니다. 소니는
전적으로 하드웨어 회사였습니다. 그러나 1995년에 이데이 씨가 소니의 최고
운영책임자로 임명되자, 그는 콘텐츠 배포를 위한 서비스 플랫폼을 개발하는
데 회사가 전념케 했습니다. 그것은 엄청난 성공을 거두었죠!
자, 그러면 제가 말하고자 했던 것으로 돌아가겠습니다. 소니처럼 우리도 우리
의 비즈니스 모델을 차별화해야 합니다. 그러면 어떻게 우리의 경쟁사들과 차
별화할 수 있을까요?

Presentation 2 발표 전개하기 p.49   22.mp3

엄청난 기회가 우리 앞에 놓여 있다는 것을 자신 있게 말씀드릴 수 있습니다.
네트워크 시대에 들어감에 따라 우리는 이 새로운 대세를 준비해야 합니다.
오늘날 우리의 경쟁자들은 완전히 다릅니다. 이제 여러분들은 삼성, LG와 같
은 회사 이름과 로고를 볼 수 있습니다. 둘 다 아시아 회사들이죠.
광대역 인터넷 기반의 보급률이 가장 높은 다섯 개 국가를 살펴봅시다. 그 다섯
나라 중 네 나라가 아시아 국가들입니다. 한국이 가장 흥미로운 허브 중의 하나
가 될 것이라는 것은 과장이 아닙니다. 이곳 사람들은 언제나 새로운 기술을 쉽
게 받아들입니다. 또한 한국은 아시아로 들어가는 관문이라는 점을 언급하고
싶습니다. 한국에서 새로운 비즈니스 모델을 개발할 기회가 있음을 여러분께
서 인지하실 수 있기를 바랍니다.

Practice 1 Let's Speak p.50

A 1 ⓒ 2 ⓓ 3 ⓑ 4 ⓐ 5 ⓔ

B 1 ⓓ, ⓗ, ⓑ, ⓖ, ⓔ 2 ⓘ, ⓐ, ⓒ, ⓕ

Practice 2 Listen-up p.51

Audio Script – A, B   23.mp3

> I would like to start my presentation by sharing our current marketing strategy with you.
> Our marketing strategy at the moment depends highly on word-of-mouth and oil quality. However, it hasn't been working fine as you can see from the chart showing our sales history. Therefore, I must mention that there must be a change in our strategy.
> Especially in the case of an oil company like us, gas station locations are really important. Let's take the example of Exxon Shell. It has 26,000 gas stations near almost all of the interstate on- and off-ramps across the nation. It is no exaggeration to say that our location strategy is a complete failure.

우리의 현 마케팅 전략을 여러분들과 공유함으로써 발표를 시작하겠습니다.
우리의 마케팅 전략은 현재 입소문과 기름의 품질에 크게 의존하고 있습니다. 그러나, 우리의 매출 이력을 보여주는 도표에서 알 수 있듯이 이러한 전략이 실효를 거두지 못하고 있습니다. 따라서 우리의 전략에 변화가 있어야 한다는 점을 말씀드려야겠습니다.
특히 우리와 같은 정유회사의 경우, 주유소의 위치는 정말 중요합니다. 엑손셀의 경우를 예로 들어보죠. 그 회사는 전국에 걸쳐 거의 모든 주간(州間) 고속도로 근방의 진출입로에 26,000개의 주유소가 있습니다. 우리의 위치 전략은 완전히 실패라고 해도 과언이 아닙니다.

A 1 Their current marketing strategy.
2 An oil company.
3 A chart showing their sales history.
4 Their location strategy.
5 26,000

B 1 by sharing 2 depends highly on
3 must mention that 4 in the case of
5 take the example 6 no exaggeration to say

Audio Script – C   24.mp3

> Have you ever wondered why everybody in this company must be a creative designer? When a customer buys a product, what do you think he or she looks at first? It's design, not technology. Customers tend to prefer products that make them feel upgraded. That's why I strongly recommend that we be a designer. Now it's time to discuss how to become a creative and innovative designer.

왜 이 회사의 모든 이가 창조적인 디자이너가 되어야만 하는지 궁금해한 적이 있습니까? 소비자가 물건을 살 때, 무엇을 가장 먼저 본다고 생각하세요?
기술이 아니라, 디자인입니다. 고객들은 자신을 빛나 보이게 하는 제품을 선호하는 경향이 있습니다. 그것이 바로 우리가 디자이너가 되어야 한다고 강하게 권유하는 이유입니다. 이제 어떻게 하면 창조적이고 혁신적인 디자이너가 될 수 있는가를 논의할 시간입니다.

C 1 False 2 False 3 True

WEEK 06 \ 발표 마무리하기 및 질문받기

Vocabulary Check-up p.53

A 1 ⓔ 2 ⓒ 3 ⓐ 4 ⓓ 5 ⓑ

B 1 concludes 2 looked at 3 clear on 4 put / briefly
5 end by

C 1 Summarizing what 2 what you said
3 conclusion / emphasize 4 Thank / for 5 questions

Presentation 1 요약하고 마무리하기 p.54   25.mp3

지금까지 말씀 드린 것을 요약해보겠습니다.
첫째, 저희는 비용 구조를 훨씬 유연하게 해놓았습니다. 따라서, 시장 수요에 반응할 수 있는 더 나은 위치에 있습니다. 둘째, 저희는 이미 운영상의 효율성 면에서 엄청난 개선을 이룩했습니다. 셋째, 저희는 최적화를 위해 우리의 잠재력을 십분 활용할 수 있도록 꾸준히 노력하고 있습니다. 이러한 것들은 저희 회사가 지난 몇 년간 쌓아놓은 역량의 증거입니다.
끝으로, 저희는 이러한 노력이 지속되도록 노력할 것입니다. 끝까지 집중해 들어주셔서 정말로 감사 드립니다. 하루 중 가장 졸음이 쏟아지는 이 시간에 깨어 있느라 노력해주신 것에 특히 감사를 표합니다.

Presentation 2 질문에 답하기 p.55   26.mp3

A: 이것으로 제 발표를 마칩니다. 지금까지 제가 말씀 드린 것에 대해 질문 있습니까?
B: 로열 박사님, 저는 크리스틴이라고 합니다. 그러면 성공적인 사업을 이루어내는 데 있어서 가장 중요한 요소들은 무엇이라고 생각하시나요?
A: 네, 아주 좋은 질문입니다. 유럽시장에서 가장 중요한 것 중 하나는 야망을 크게 갖는 것이라고 생각해요. 그러나 무엇보다도 현실적이어야 하죠.
B: 무슨 뜻인지 모르겠습니다.
A: 미안합니다, 아마도 제가 명확하게 말씀을 못 드린 것 같군요. 영국에서 최고의 서적 판매업자가 되고 싶다고 가정해봅시다. 그러나 포부를 이루기 위해서는 영국 시장과 관련된 위험 요소들을 현실적으로 분석해야 하죠.
B: 그 말에 전적으로 동의합니다.
A: 감사합니다. 질문 더 있으신가요? 더 이상 질문이 없으면 여기서 마치도록 하겠습니다.

Practice 1 Let's Speak p.56

A 1 That concludes my demonstration of our new software.
2 Thank you so much for your attention.
3 I don't see what you mean.
4 Let me sum up what we have just discussed so far.
5 Are there any questions on what I've told you all so far?
6 If there are no further questions, I'd like to stop here.

B 1 ⓓ, ⓑ, ⓒ 2 ⓐ, ⓕ, ⓔ

Practice 2 Listen-up p.57

Audio Script – A, B 27.mp3

> Now let me sum up my presentation with an outlook for our business.
> First, we are one of the global leaders in the health food business. Second, we have a very strong asset base with superior technology in the latest product generation. There is no doubt that we, VegeTwo, are one of the innovation drivers. Third, 50 years of tradition and industrial knowledge as a leading company enable us to quickly respond to market requirements.
> In conclusion, we always keep track of the global market mega trends in order to ensure long-term success. Thank you.

이제 저희 사업의 전망과 함께 제 발표를 요약하도록 하겠습니다.
첫째, 저희는 건강식품 사업에서 글로벌 리더 중 하나입니다. 둘째, 최신 제품 개발에 있어 우수한 기술 베이스가 있습니다. 우리 VegeTwo가 혁신 추진원 중의 하나라는 것은 의심의 여지가 없습니다. 셋째, 선도 기업으로서 50년간 축적된 전통과 업계 지식으로 우리는 시장 요구에 빠르게 대응할 수 있습니다.
끝으로, 저희는 장기적인 성공을 보장하기 위해 언제나 글로벌 시장의 대세를 주시하고 있습니다. 감사합니다.

A 1 False 2 True 3 True 4 False

B 1 let me sum up 2 First 3 Second
4 There is no doubt 5 Third 6 as a leading company
7 In conclusion 8 in order to

Audio Script – C 28.mp3

> A And that's it. Are there any comments or questions?
> B Thank you very much for the presentation and also for being here, Mr. Wilson. Does your company have a view or a position on this newest technology?
> A How much longer do we have?
> B As much time as you like.
> A It is almost impossible to get an official view, stance, etc, at the moment. However, I'd like to point out that there was a joint workshop in Stockholm where we found out that this biotechnology was very stable and very safe.
> C When are you planning to use this technology commercially?
> A Our engineers are working on developing a new product equipped with that technology. We anticipate it will be done by September. Are there any more questions? If there are no further questions, I think we should stop here.

> A 이게 끝입니다. 논평이나 질문 있으세요?
> B 여기까지 와주셔서 발표해주셔서 감사 드립니다, 윌슨 씨. 이 최신 기술에 대한 귀사의 입장이나 견해가 있으신지요?
> A 시간이 얼마나 더 있죠?
> B 원하는 만큼 하시면 됩니다.
> A 지금 당장 공식적인 견해나 입장을 취하는 것은 매우 어렵습니다. 하지만 스톡홀름에서 가진 공동워크숍에서 이 생명공학기술이 매우 안정적이고 안전하다는 것이 밝혀졌다는 점을 지적하고 싶군요.
> C 이 기술을 언제 상업적으로 이용할 계획이세요?
> A 우리 기술자들이 새로운 기술이 장착된 신제품을 개발 중에 있습니다. 9월까지는 끝날 것으로 예상하고 있어요. 다른 질문 더 있으세요? 추가 질문이 없으면, 여기서 마치도록 하겠습니다.

C 1 the newest technology
2 the joint workshop
3 September

PLUS WEEK \ 시각자료 사용 및 효과적인 분석

Vocabulary Check-up p.59

A 1 © 2 ⓐ 3 ⓔ 4 ⓑ 5 ⓓ

B 1 increased by 2 represents 3 concentrate on
4 slowed down 5 take a look / see

C 1 horizontal axis / vertical axis 2 row 3 In comparison
4 As / result 5 soared to

Presentation 1 시각자료 활용하기 p.60 29.mp3

여러분께 보여드릴 차트가 몇 개 있습니다.
이 막대 그래프를 보면 작년에 마케팅보다 연구개발에 더 많은 돈을 지출했다는 것을 알 수 있습니다. 화면에 나와 있는 차트에서 알 수 있듯이, 재작년과 비교해서 30% 증가된 1,000달러를 연구개발에 썼습니다. 반면에 마케팅 투자 비용은 30% 감소했습니다.
그러나 이제는 우리 제품을 사람들에게 알리기 위해 마케팅에 좀 더 집중해야 할 때입니다. 이 선 그래프를 보시죠. 우리 경쟁사들의 마케팅 투자액을 보여주고 있습니다. 그들은 우리가 작년에 마케팅에 투자했던 것의 거의 두 배에 해당하는 돈을 썼습니다.

Presentation 2 효과적으로 분석하기 p.61 30.mp3

일본 시장에 새롭게 진입했음에도 불구하고 우리의 매출은 꾸준합니다. 반면에, 우리 경쟁업체들 대부분은 매출을 끌어올리는 데 어려움을 겪고 있습니다. 영업부에서 올라온 보고서에 따르면, 우리는 작년 한 해에만 1천5백 대의 자동차를 판매했습니다.
그런 그렇고, 제가 나누어드린 인쇄물을 봐주시겠습니까? 인쇄물에 나온 도표에서 볼 수 있듯이, 중국에서의 판매가 1년 전에 비해 30%가 떨어졌습니다. 일본 시장과는 대조적으로 중국에서의 매출이 둔화되었습니다.
하지만 중국에서의 낮은 매출에 대해 걱정할 필요는 없습니다. 아실지도 모르겠지만, 올해 말에 중국에 마케팅 사무소를 열 계획입니다. 그 직접적인 결과로서, 우리는 중국 시장에서도 수익을 창출할 수 있을 것으로 기대하고 있습니다.

Practice 1 Let's Speak p.62

A
1 Please take a look at the chart on the screen.
2 These numbers are based on the report from our customer service center.
3 The defective goods have increased while sales have dropped.
4 According to a survey, people are watching movies twice a week.
5 I'd like us to pay attention to the dotted line, which represents the consumption of rice.

B 1 ⓔ, ⓐ, ⓒ, ⓓ 2 ⓑ, ⓗ, ⓕ, ⓖ

Practice 2 Listen-up p.63

Audio Script – A 31.mp3

I'd like to show you some bar graphs, which can show you a good indicator for choosing a network company. Now let's take a look at the first graph. The vertical axis shows the number of audience members who visit the corresponding network every day. The horizontal axis represents the networks. AceWeb is in the lead. And it is followed by Yazoo, Macrosoft, MSM, and LOA. There is a gap of roughly 25 million people between first and last place.

But you may not have wanted to go with total audience. Instead, if you are considering using page views, then look at the second graph next to the first one. It indicates that MSM is your network of choice. It is followed by AceWeb, LOA, Yazoo, and Macrosoft. In this case, there is a roughly 3 billion page view difference between first and last place.

네트워크 회사를 선택하는 데 있어 좋은 지표를 보여주는 막대 그래프를 몇 개 보여드리겠습니다.

자, 첫 번째 그래프를 보시죠. 세로축은 매일 해당 네트워크를 방문하는 사람들의 수를 나타냅니다. 가로축은 네트워크들을 나타내고 있고요. 에이스웹이 선두입니다. 그 뒤로 야주, 매크로소프트, MSM, LOA가 뒤따르고 있습니다. 선두와 최하위 사이에는 대략 2천5백만 명의 차이가 있습니다.

하지만 전체 방문자 수로 따지고 싶지 않을 수도 있습니다. 그 대신 페이지 조회수를 고려한다면, 첫 번째 그래프 옆에 있는 두 번째 그래프를 봐주세요. MSM이 당신이 선택해야 할 네트워크라는 걸 보여주는군요. 그 뒤를 에이스웹, LOA, 야주, 매크로소프트가 뒤따르고 있네요. 이 경우에는, 선두와 최하위 사이에 대략 30억의 페이지 조회수 차이가 있습니다.

A 1 25 2 3

Audio Script – B, C 32.mp3

Our television news programs are in trouble with the American public. According to our survey, the viewership of our nightly news has been particularly hard hit. In contrast, the percentage of people who listen to radio news programs is largely the same as it has been over the past three years.

We believe that the decline in TV news viewing may be related to the increasing use of smartphones. However, listening to radio news, which usually occurs while doing some other tasks, did not decline among smartphone users.

우리의 텔레비전 뉴스 프로그램은 미국 대중들 사이에서 그리 인기가 없습니다. 설문조사에 의하면, 저녁 뉴스 시청률이 특히 저조합니다. 대조적으로, 라디오 뉴스 프로그램을 듣는 사람들의 비율은 과거 3년 동안에도 그랬듯이 거의 그대로입니다.

TV 뉴스 시청률의 감소는 스마트폰의 사용 증가와 관련이 있다고 봅니다. 하지만, 보통 다른 일을 하면서 라디오 뉴스를 듣는 건 스마트폰 사용자들 사이에서 줄지 않았습니다.

B 1 True 2 False 3 True

C 1 According to our survey 2 In contrast
3 We believe that 4 may be related to
5 did not decline

WEEK 07 \ 업무 지시하기 및 협조 요청하기

Vocabulary Check-up p.69

A 1 ⓑ 2 ⓓ 3 ⓔ 4 ⓐ 5 ⓒ

B 1 like you 2 Would you 3 any help 4 Be sure
5 trouble you

C 1 give / hand 2 analyze 3 a favor 4 take over
5 have / minutes

Conversation 1 업무 지시하기 p.70 33.mp3

A: 이번 달 말까지 끝마쳐야 할 몇 가지 업무들이 있어요. 모두들 알다시피, 우리 신제품에 대한 고객만족도 조사를 실시할 겁니다. 켈리, 그것을 당신한테 맡겨도 될까요?

B: 좋습니다. 제가 하겠습니다.

A: 잭, 2월 판매 보고서를 작성해주세요.

C: 알겠습니다.

A: 노라, 당신은 오늘 오후에 고객 미팅에 참석해주세요.

D: 죄송합니다, 페라로 씨. 오늘은 스케줄이 꽉 찼어요. 그래서 아무래도 미팅에 참석할 수 없겠는데요.

A: 그렇군요. 그러면 대신 제가 참석하죠. 자, 됐습니다. 일들 합시다!

Conversation 2 도움 요청하기 p.71 34.mp3

A: 폴, 바빠? 부탁 하나 들어줄래?

B: 뭔데?

A: 오늘 오후에 회의가 있어. 나 대신에 마케팅 보고서 나머지를 끝내줄래? 바로 처리해야 할 다른 일이 있거든.

B: 사실 지금 무척 바쁜데.

A: 좀 도와줘, 폴.

B: 흠, 설마 내가 하루 종일 이 일에 매달리기를 기대하는 것은 아니겠지?

A: 아니지. 끝내는 데 그리 오래 걸리지는 않을 거야.

B: 흠⋯ 그러면 할 수 있을 것 같은데. 하지만 나한테 큰 신세 진 거야.

Practice 1 Let's Speak p.72

A 1 take / urgent 2 favor / full 3 give / hand
4 like / please

B 1 How's the show preparation going? /
What's wrong with them? /
I'd like you to repair them as soon as possible.
2 But I can't get this projector to work. /
Can I call a technician to take a look at it?

Practice 2 Listen-up p.73

Audio Script – A, B 35.mp3

David	You look depressed. What's up, Jade?
Jade	I just spoke with my client over the phone. He wants to advance the opening date of the website to June 6. So, I should clear my schedule after work this week.
David	That's too bad. Would you like me to help you with that?
Jade	Really? It would be a huge help, David.
David	What do you want me to do first?
Jade	Can I leave it to you to test the beta version of the website?
David	No problem.
Jade	Thanks, David.
David	That's what colleagues are for.

데이비드 우울해 보이는데요. 무슨 일이에요, 제이드?

제이드 방금 고객과 통화했는데, 웹사이트 공개 일을 6월 6일로 앞당기고 싶대요. 그래서 이번 주에는 근무 후의 일정을 취소해야 해요.

데이비드 안됐네요. 그거 제가 좀 도와줄까요?

제이드 정말요? 큰 도움이 될 거예요, 데이비드.

데이비드 먼저 뭐부터 할까요?

제이드 웹사이트의 베타 버전 테스트를 맡겨도 될까요?

데이비드 좋아요.

제이드 고마워요, 데이비드.

데이비드 그래서 동료가 좋다는 거죠.

A 1 ⓑ 2 ⓐ

B 1 look depressed 2 advance the opening date
3 clear my schedule 4 to help you with that
5 It would be a huge help 6 Can I leave it to you

Audio Script – C 36.mp3

Since we have a training workshop early next month, I'd like to divide our roles so that we can prepare efficiently. Jeff, I'd like you to check how many people will attend it by the end of the week. Andy, since you are the host of the workshop, please inform me about its procedure in writing by next week. Maria, please make sure that we have all the equipment necessary for the workshop. It would be great if you could make a list of the items needed so that you won't miss anything.

다음 달 초에 교육 워크숍이 있어서 우리의 역할을 나눠서 효율적으로 준비하려고 합니다. 제프, 이번 주말까지 몇 명이 참석할지 파악해주세요. 앤디, 당신이 워크숍 사회자니까 다음 주까지 문서로 진행 절차를 알려주세요. 마리아, 워크숍에 필요한 장비를 모두 갖출 수 있도록 확인해주세요. 필요한 품목의 목록을 만든다면 아주 좋겠죠. 그러면 빠뜨리는 물건이 없을 테니까요.

C 1 False 2 False 3 True 4 True

WEEK 08 \ 업무 진행 상황 체크하기

Vocabulary Check-up p.75

A 1 ⓑ 2 ⓒ 3 ⓔ 4 ⓐ 5 ⓓ

B 1 bring forward 2 better finish 3 ahead of
4 slightly later 5 our best

C 1 as fast 2 status 3 When / done[finished/completed]
4 out of time 5 far

Conversation 1 진행 상황 파악하기 p.76 37.mp3

A: 제인, 매출 보고서 작성을 끝마쳤나요?
B: 거의 끝났습니다. 하지만 하반기 매출 수치는 여전히 작업 중입니다.
A: 오늘까지가 마감인 것으로 알고 있는데요.
B: 알고 있는데요, 예산 제안서를 쓰느라고 바빴습니다. 이틀 더 시간을 주실 수 있을까요? 목요일까지 최선을 다해 끝내도록 하겠습니다.
A: 금요일에 이사회 회의가 있어요. 거기서 매출 실적을 보고하도록 되어 있어요. 그때까지는 최종본이 필요합니다.
B: 알겠습니다. 걱정하지 마세요.

Conversation 2 시간 관리와 마감일 p.77 38.mp3

A: 새로운 웹사이트의 문제들이 언제 해결될 거라고 보고 있나요?
B: 11월 초를 목표로 하고 있습니다. 하지만 그보다 더 빠를 수도 약간 늦을 수도 있어요.
A: 11월 말까지 가동시킬 수 있으면 좋겠는데요.
B: 후원사들의 배너로 웹사이트를 링크시키는 것이 생각보다 무척 어렵네요. 하지만 거의 다 끝나가요.
A: 알지 모르겠는데, 12월 1일에 신규 고객들과 중요한 미팅이 있어요. 그래서 새 웹사이트에 접근할 수 있으면 상황이 훨씬 더 쉬워질 거예요.
B: 물론이죠. 신규 고객들에게 좋은 인상을 심어주는 것이 절대적으로 중요하다는 것을 알고 있어요. 최선을 다하고 있습니다. 현재 웹사이트가 우리의 최우선 사항입니다.

Practice 1 Let's Speak p.78

A 1 over / take 2 best / by 3 complete / fast
4 sure / on

B 1 It's almost done. / We're doing our best. / please finish it by the end of this month at the latest.
2 how far along are you with the report? / It looks like you are ahead of schedule.

Practice 2 Listen-up p.79

Audio Script – A, B 39.mp3

Lisa	Michael, I thought you were going to London to work on the project. What happened?
Michael	I didn't realize my visa had expired!
Lisa	Shame on you! Don't you know how important the project is?
Michael	I know, Lisa. I applied for a renewal of my visa this morning.
Lisa	When do you think it will be done?
Michael	I'm aiming for early next week. However, it may be slightly later than that.
Lisa	Do whatever is needed to get it done more quickly!

리사	마이클, 프로젝트 진행을 위해 런던으로 갈 거라 생각했어요. 어떻게 된 거예요?
마이클	비자가 만료된 것을 몰랐어요!
리사	그게 무슨 창피예요! 그 프로젝트가 얼마나 중요한지 몰라요?
마이클	알아요, 리사. 오늘 아침에 비자 갱신을 신청했어요.
리사	언제 갱신이 될 것 같아요?
마이클	다음 주 초를 목표로 하고 있어요. 하지만 그보다 조금 늦어질 수도 있어요.
리사	더 빨리 끝낼 수 있게 할 수 있는 것은 다 하세요!

A 1 His visa has expired. 2 In London.
3 He applied for a visa renewal. 4 boss

B 1 thought you were going to
2 how important the project is
3 applied for a renewal 4 it will be done
5 may be slightly later 6 get it done more quickly

Audio Script – C 40.mp3

A	When do you think the preparation for the Nagoya engineering meeting will be done?
B	Have you heard about Jeremy?
A	Nope. What happened to him?
B	He had heart surgery this morning.
A	Really? How did it go?
B	Fortunately, it went fine.
A	That's great to hear.
B	However, there will be a little delay in preparing for the meeting. He was supposed to write the product specifications.
A	When will he be able to come back to work?
B	I have no idea. Anyway, we should postpone the meeting.
A	Can you call him on his mobile and ask when he will be ready to come in?
B	Okay, I will.

A 나고야 엔지니어링 회의 준비가 언제 끝날 것 같아요?

B 제레미 얘기 들었어요?

A 아니요. 제레미한테 무슨 일이 있었어요?

B 오늘 아침에 심장 수술을 받았대요.

A 정말요? 어떻게 됐어요?

B 다행히 잘 됐답니다.

A 다행이네요.

B 하지만 회의 준비하는 게 약간 지연될 겁니다. 제레미가 제품 사양을 작성하기로 했었거든요.

A 그가 언제 업무에 복귀할 수 있을까요?

B 모르겠어요. 어쨌든 회의를 뒤로 미뤄야겠어요.

A 제레미한테 휴대전화로 전화해서 언제 출근할 수 있는지 물어봐 줄래요?

B 네, 그럴게요.

C 1 False 2 True 3 False 4 False

WEEK 09 \ 문제에 대한 논의 및 해결

Vocabulary Check-up p.81

A 1 ⓑ 2 ⓔ 3 ⓒ 4 ⓐ 5 ⓓ

B 1 trouble with 2 related to 3 do with 4 work out
5 Make sure

C 1 solution 2 Has / reported 3 resulted from
4 investigate 5 root cause

Conversation 1 문제 보고하기 p.82   41.mp3

A: 펠릭스, 고객으로부터 불만사항을 접수했습니다.

B: 정말이에요? 자세히 설명해주실래요?

A: 약 일주일 전에 그 여자 고객이 우리 스피커를 하나 샀어요. 잘 작동되는데, 이따금 강한 고음의 소리가 몇 초간 지속되다가 없어진답니다. 귀가 정말 아프다고 하네요.

B: 흠... 전에도 이 문제가 보고된 적이 있나요?

A: 이런 기술적인 결함에 대해서는 들은 적이 없습니다.

B: 그 고객은 무엇을 원하던가요? 환불을 원하나요, 제품 교환을 원하나요?

A: 환불이요.

B: 그 불량 스피커를 회수해서 앞으로 그런 일이 다시 발생하지 않도록 근본적인 원인을 파악하도록 하세요.

Conversation 2 문제 논의 및 해결하기 p.83   42.mp3

A: 모든 것을 시도했지만 방화벽을 작동시킬 수가 없네요. 처음엔 설치된 소프트웨어에 문제가 있다고 생각했어요. 하지만 이걸 보세요. 소프트웨어는 아주 잘 작동하고 있잖아요.

B: 패치 프로그램을 설치했어요?

A: 물론이죠. 사용자 매뉴얼대로 했어요.

B: 그러면 뭐가 문제죠?

A: 아주 신경 쓰이네요. 제가 걱정하는 건 누군가가 우리 인트라넷을 해킹할 수도 있다는 것이에요.

B: 기다렸다가 내일 아침에 IT 보안회사에 전화해보는 것이 어떨까요? 필요하다면 우리를 도와줄 기술자를 보내줄 거예요.

A: 네. 그게 이 시점에서 우리가 할 수 있는 유일한 일이네요.

Practice 1 Let's Speak p.84

A 1 ⓓ 2 ⓔ 3 ⓕ 4 ⓒ 5 ⓐ 6 ⓑ

B 1 We received a complaint from one of our customers. /
I think it has something to do with the batteries. /
find out the root cause of the problem
2 What makes you think we have a problem with the server? /
have one of them take a look at your computer

Practice 2 Listen-up p.85

Audio Script – A, B   43.mp3

Kevin Mr. Brasher just called and said he's stuck in bad traffic now.

Rachel No way! We were supposed to go over our presentation with him. How long did he say it would take to get here?

Kevin He said he won't be able to make it to the meeting considering the traffic conditions. Why don't we start without him?

Rachel My concern is that he has all the documents needed for the meeting. I don't know what to do.

Kevin How about asking him to send the documents by email?

Rachel That's a good idea.

케빈 브래셔 씨한테 방금 전화 왔는데 현재 교통체증 때문에 꼼짝 못 한대요.

레이첼 이럴 수가! 그와 함께 프레젠테이션 검토하기로 돼있는데. 여기 도착하는 데 얼마나 걸린대요?

케빈 교통상황을 고려하면 회의 참가가 불가능할 거라고 하네요. 그냥 그 사람 없이 시작하는 게 어때요?

레이첼 제가 걱정하는 건 그가 회의에 필요한 모든 자료를 갖고 있다는 점이에요. 어떻게 해야 할지 모르겠군요.

케빈 이메일로 문서들을 보내달라고 하면 어떨까요?

레이첼 그거 좋은 생각이네요.

A 1 True 2 False 3 False

B 1 stuck in bad traffic 2 We were supposed to
3 would take to get here 4 won't be able to make it
5 needed for the meeting 6 How about asking him

A Terry told me the blueprints will be ready by Tuesday instead of Monday.

B Oh, no. That means we might have to postpone our meeting with the contractors on Tuesday.

A Well, I think if he works a few extra hours this weekend, he can get things done.

B Oh, I see. Can you ask him if he has anything planned for this weekend?

A Okay, I will.

B How about you, Molly? Do you have something to do this weekend? If you don't, I hope you can help him then.

A Actually, Saturday is my son's birthday, so I'm hosting a party for him.

A 테리가 그 청사진들이 월요일이 아니라 화요일까지 준비될 수 있다고 했어요.

B 아, 안 돼요. 그러면 화요일에 있을 계약업체들과의 미팅을 연기해야 한다는 얘기잖아요.

A 음, 그가 주말에 몇 시간 더 근무한다면 일을 끝낼 수 있을 거예요.

B 아, 그렇군요. 이번 주말에 다른 계획된 일이 없는지 테리한테 좀 물어봐 줄래요?

A 네, 그럴게요.

B 당신은 어때요, 몰리? 이번 주말에 할 일 있어요? 없으면 테리를 도왔으면 하는데요.

A 사실, 토요일이 아들 생일이라서 제가 파티를 열거든요.

C 1 The blueprints won't be ready on time.
2 They might have to postpone a meeting.
3 Working on the weekend.
4 She is hosting a party for her son.

PLUS WEEK \ 스트레스 관리 및 자기계발

Vocabulary Check-up p.87

A 1 ⓑ 2 ⓔ 3 ⓓ 4 ⓐ 5 ⓒ

B 1 stressed out 2 under stress 3 regular basis
4 keeps pressuring 5 get rid

C 1 diet / fit 2 make / rule 3 class / Spanish
4 exercise regularly 5 relieves[reduces] / by

Conversation 1 스트레스에 대해 이야기하기 p.88   45.mp3

A: 그가 내일까지 보고서를 끝내라고 압력을 넣고 있어요. 그의 태도를 참을 수가 없어요!

B: 진정해요, 신디. 압박은 모든 일의 일부분이고 우리가 일하도록 동기 유발을 해주거든요.

A: 하지만 그 사람은 성공에 안달이 나서 주위 사람들 모두를 괴롭히잖아요. 모든 사람들이 자기를 피하려 한다는 걸 그는 모르는 것 같아요.

B: 네, 알아요. 그 사람은 자기가 항상 옳다고 생각하고 자기 의견만 중요한 것처럼 행동하죠. 하지만, 과도한 압박은 스트레스로 이어져 업무 성과를 떨어뜨린다고 들었어요.

A: 의심의 여지가 없는 말이에요. 토드, 이제 그 얘기는 그만하죠. 더 스트레스만 받으니까요.

Conversation 2 자기 계발과 건강 관리 p.89   46.mp3

A: 회사가 직장 내 자기 계발을 위한 교육 프로그램을 운영할 것이라는 얘기 들었어요?

B: 정말이에요? 그거 재미있겠는데요. 무엇을 배우게 되나요?

A: 경영진은 내년에 사업을 해외로 확장할 계획이에요. 그래서 영어를, 특히 비즈니스 환경에서 할 수 있도록 우리를 교육시키고자 해요. 우리가 전자 학습 모듈을 끝내게 될 거예요.

B: 그거 좋은 생각 같은데요. 전자학습이면 언제 어디서든지 배우는 것이 가능하잖아요.

A: 맞아요. 그건 그렇고, 당신 매일 야근한다고 들었어요. 건강은 어떻게 챙기세요?

B: 사실, 아침 5시에 일어나서 회사 헬스클럽으로 간답니다. 보통 사무실로 가기 전에 한 시간 정도 운동을 해요. 그것 때문에 활기 있게 사는 거죠.

Practice 1 Let's Speak p.90

A 1 This program makes it possible for us to pick up new skills quickly.
2 He keeps pressuring me not to take sick leave.
3 He put pressure on us to get the work done faster.
4 We are having a workshop on a regular basis to improve our work efficiency.

B 1 Are you stressed out these days? / Why aren't you enjoying the fresh air and stretching out?
2 I exercise at a health club for about an hour. / I learn Chinese online at home.

Audio Script – A, B   47.mp3

Josh	How can I eliminate stress from my life?
Emily	Why? What's up with you?
Josh	My boss keeps pressuring me to work overtime until my job is finished. He's acting like a dictator. Tell me how I can manage stress better?
Emily	I feel sorry for you, Josh. You should learn to moderate your physical reactions to stress. Slow, deep breathing will bring your respiration back to normal. It works for me. Give it a go, man.
Josh	No, I just fancy a drink.

조쉬	삶의 스트레스를 어떻게 하면 날려버릴 수 있을까?
에밀리	왜? 무슨 일이야?
조쉬	상사가 일이 끝날 때까지 야근하라고 계속 난리야. 독재자처럼 군다고. 어떻게 하면 스트레스를 더 잘 관리할 수 있을까?
에밀리	안됐군, 조쉬. 스트레스에 대한 당신의 신체적 반응을 완화시키는 법을 배워야 해. 느리고 깊게 숨을 쉬면 호흡이 정상으로 돌아가지. 난 효과가 있더라. 한 번 해봐.
조쉬	아니야, 난 그저 술이나 한잔하고 싶을 뿐이야.

A 1 False 2 True 3 False 4 True

B 1 eliminate stress 2 keeps pressuring me
3 manage stress better
4 moderate your physical reactions
5 It works for me

Audio Script – C   48.mp3

A	I've got to learn to use the features of Microsoft Excel to quickly create great-looking spreadsheets.
B	Why is that, Rachel?
A	I'm transferring to the Accounting Department next month. You know how important it is to use Microsoft Excel in an efficient manner.
B	Oh, I didn't know that.
A	Anyway, do you know where I can pick up those skills?
B	Don't you know we have an in-house website where you can learn those things? Just go to www.tgl.com.
A	That sounds interesting. Thank you for the good advice!

A	훌륭한 워크시트를 빠르게 만들려면 엑셀 기능 사용법을 배워야 할 것 같은데.
B	그건 왜, 레이첼?
A	다음 달에 회계부서로 옮겨. 효율적으로 엑셀을 사용하는 것이 얼마나 중요한지 알잖아.
B	어, 몰랐던 사실이네.
A	아무튼, 어디서 그런 기술을 배울 수 있는지 알아?
B	그런 걸 배울 수 있는 사내 웹사이트가 있다는 것 몰랐어? www.tgl.com으로 가봐.
A	그거 흥미로운데. 좋은 조언 고마워!

C 1 ⓒ 2 ⓓ 3 ⓑ

PART 4

효과적인 의사 표현
Expressing Opinions Effectively

WEEK 10 \ 의견 교환 및 상호 신뢰

Vocabulary Check-up p.97

A 1 ⓑ 2 ⓓ 3 ⓔ 4 ⓐ 5 ⓒ

B 1 understand / position 2 little wonder
   3 some reason 4 too much 5 no doubt

C 1 trust / under 2 rely[depend] / help 3 confidence
   4 Everyone wants 5 Nobody knows

Conversation 1 분명하게 의견 표현하기 p.98   49.mp3

A: 고객으로서 특별하게 대접받는 것이 정말 좋아요. 상점에 들어서면 직원이
   정중하게 내게 문을 열어주길 바라죠.

B: 그건 모든 고객들이 원하는 거죠. 누가 푸대접 받기를 원하겠어요?

A: 재정적으로 곤란을 겪는 회사들은 보통 형편 없는 고객 서비스를 하더군
   요.

B: 맞아요. 그런데 우리 회사는 단지 제품과 돈 버는 것에만 집중하고 있어요.
   우리가 경쟁사들에게 고객을 잃고 있는 게 이상한 일도 아니죠.

A: 훌륭한 서비스가 더 많은 고객을 끌어들인다는 것을 어떻게 경영진이 모를
   수가 있을까요? 여전히 고객들이 사용 설명서를 읽도록 만든다는 것을 믿
   을 수가 없어요. 전화상으로 차근차근 제품 사용 방법을 설명해야 해요.

Conversation 2 이해와 신뢰 표현하기 p.99   50.mp3

A: 협상은 어떻게 됐어요?

B: 결국 새로운 계약에 합의하지 못했어요. 우린 더 많은 봉급을 받길 원해요.
   그래서 파업을 생각 중이에요.

A: 당신들이 충분히 그럴 만하다고 생각해요. 하지만, 경영진이 당신들의 요
   구를 받아들이기엔 너무 어렵지 않을까요? 우리 회사가 심각하게 절하된
   주가로 고생하고 있잖아요. 임금 인상을 얘기하기에는 시기가 안 좋아요.

B: 알아요. 그래서 재정 문제를 함께 해결한 후에 재협상하자고 했어요. 우리
   관계는 서로에 대한 신뢰와 존중에 바탕을 두어야 한다는 것을 알기 때문
   이죠.

Practice 1 Let's Speak p.100

A 1 little wonder 2 How / possibly 3 bad timing
   4 go / well

B 1 I can't believe we're still using a typewriter.
   2 I've always trusted in him and left important projects
     to him.

Practice 2 Listen-up p.101

Audio Script – A   51.mp3

A   Hey, Todd. Can you come over here for just a minute?
    I'd like to get your opinion on these company logo
    samples.
B   Sure, with pleasure. Let me see…
A   What do you think about this shape in red?
B   Who would love that ill-matched logo?
A   Hmm… How about the green logo then?
B   I think it stands out and really captures my attention.
A   Sorry, I don't get it.
B   It's eye-catching.
A   Isn't it too bright?
B   No, I think the green color helps enhance the design.
    The design company did a really nice job on the logo.
    They deserve their reputation.

A   이봐요, 토드. 잠시만 이리로 와볼래요? 이 회사 로고 샘플들에 대해 당신 의견
    을 듣고 싶어요.
B   그러죠. 어디 볼까요….
A   빨간색이 들어간 이 모양은 어떻게 생각하세요?
B   누가 그렇게 잘못 매치된 로고를 좋아하겠어요?
A   음… 그럼 이 녹색 로고는 어때요?
B   두드러지는 게 시선을 확 잡아 끄는 것 같네요.
A   죄송하지만, 무슨 말씀인지 잘 모르겠어요.
B   눈길을 끈다고요.
A   너무 밝지 않나요?
B   아니요, 녹색이 디자인을 강화해주는 것 같은데요. 그 디자인 회사가 로고 작업
    을 정말 잘 했네요. 평판이 좋을 만해요.

A 1 ⓑ 2 ⓒ 3 ⓐ

Audio Script – B, C   52.mp3

Thomson	Linda, are you finished with the budget projections?
Linda	I'm not. I'm still working on them. When do you need them by, Mr. Thomson?
Thomson	I'll need them by Tuesday to look over so I can give them to Emma by Wednesday.
Linda	Don't worry. I'm almost finished.
Thomson	I really appreciate that. You know, I always thank you for the sweet things you've done for me, Linda.
Linda	Don't mention it, Mr. Thomson. Actually, I'd like to thank you for always trusting me.

164

톰슨　린다, 예산 계획 다 끝냈어요?

린다　아뇨. 아직 작업 중이에요. 언제까지 필요한데요, 톰슨 씨?

톰슨　수요일까지 엠마에게 전해줘야 하니까 검토하려면 화요일까지 필요해요.

린다　걱정 말아요. 거의 끝나가요.

톰슨　정말 고마워요. 있잖아요. 항상 날 위해 해주는 일들에 고마워하고 있어요, 린다.

린다　그런 말 마세요, 톰슨 씨. 사실 항상 절 신뢰해주셔서 감사하고 있는 걸요.

B　1 True　2 False　3 False　4 True

C　1 are you finished with　2 by Tuesday to look over
3 really appreciate that　4 like to thank you for

WEEK 11 ＼ 추측과 확신 및 불평과 이해

Vocabulary Check-up p.103

A　1 ⓔ　2 ⓐ　3 ⓓ　4 ⓒ　5 ⓑ

B　1 obvious　2 sure　3 might　4 unlikely
5 firmly believe

C　1 say / confidence　2 fed up with　3 see / getting
4 complains[grumbles]　5 sense

Conversation 1 추측과 확신 p.104　53.mp3

A: 사람들이 우리 샌드위치를 먹고 탈이 났어요.

B: 그럴 수가! 식중독을 계속 주의해 왔잖아요, 그렇지 않나요?

A: 그래요. 그런데 땅콩버터에 문제가 있었던 것 같아요. 땅콩버터 일부가 홍수로 인한 전력차단 때문에 상한 게 틀림없어요.

B: 어떻게 이런 일이 있을 수 있죠? 이 일로 회사의 명성에 먹칠할 수도 있다고요.

A: 언제 이 문제가 보도될지 모르겠지만, 손해를 최소화할 조치를 취해야 해요.

B: 뭐 좋은 생각이라도 있어요?

A: 즉시 공개 사과문을 발표해야 한다고 확신합니다.

Conversation 2 불평과 이해 p.105　54.mp3

A: 하루 종일 사무실에 처박혀 있는 게 정말 지긋지긋해요! 내 상사를 봐요. 만날 고객들과 저녁 먹으러 나가잖아요.

B: 음, 저스틴, 이런 말 하고 싶진 않지만 임원들은 스트레스를 더 많이 받아요.

A: 그건 당신 생각이죠, 올리비아. 그 사람들은 회사 차도 있고, 밤 늦게까지 일할 필요도 없잖아요. 게다가 봉급은 우리보다 훨씬 많고요.

B: 하지만 때론 그들이 항상 중요한 의사결정을 해야 한다는 것을 이해해줄 필요가 있어요. 게다가 팀원들도 신경 써야 하니 그게 얼마나 스트레스 받는 일인데요.

A: 불공평하다는 내 생각엔 변함이 없어요.

Practice 1 Let's Speak p.106

A　1 convinced　2 like　3 stand　4 times

B　1 I don't think he's likely to stay very long. /
I firmly believe that he would manage well.

2 It looks like he is overwhelmed by a lot of work. /
I understand what you mean

Practice 2 Listen-up p.107

Audio Script – A, B　55.mp3

Hailey　At the rate we're going, it is clear that we're going to have a much bigger company.

Joshua　You've got it all wrong. We might be in the red.

Hailey　I'm really sick and tired of your pessimism! What makes you think that?

Joshua　As you know, our company is not financially sound at the moment. How can we possibly buy another company with financial problems while we are in trouble? That will definitely ruin our company.

Hailey　Don't fret, Joshua. I firmly believe that we could generate synergy by acquiring it.

Joshua　You're not listening to me, Hailey.

헤일리　이런 식으로 가면 회사가 더 커질 것이라는 것은 자명합니다.

조슈아　전혀 잘못 알고 있네요. 적자를 보게 될지도 몰라요.

헤일리　당신의 비관적인 태도에 정말 싫증이 나요! 왜 그렇게 생각하는데요?

조슈아　알다시피 우리 회사가 지금은 재정적으로 건실하지 못하잖아요. 곤경에 처한 상황에서 어떻게 재정에 문제가 있는 또 다른 회사를 인수할 수가 있어요? 두말할 것 없이 회사를 망치는 일이에요.

헤일리　걱정 마요, 조슈아. 저는 그 회사를 인수함으로써 시너지를 창출할 것이라 굳게 믿어요.

조슈아　제 말을 안 듣는군요, 헤일리.

A　1 True　2 False　3 False

B　1 it is clear that　2 We might be　3 sick and tired of
4 How can we possibly buy　5 That will definitely
6 I firmly believe

Audio Script – C　56.mp3

A　I heard Chris has been promoted to sales manager. That means he broke the record and has become the youngest manger in this company. Isn't that so cool?

B　Hmm... I just think it's quite unfair.

A　Why? I didn't know that you thought that.

B　He's been with this company as a sales representative for only one year. How could he get promoted to that position in such a short period?

A　I see what you're getting at. However, he's been doing a great job so far. Sales have been considerably increasing since he joined the company. I'd say he deserves it.

B　That's what you think. This will leave many workers depressed.

A 크리스가 영업부장으로 승진했다고 들었어요. 그 말은 그가 기록을 깨고 이 회사에서 최연소 부장이 됐다는 거예요. 정말 신선하지 않아요?

B 음… 저는 아주 불공평하다고 봐요.

A 왜요? 그렇게 생각하시는 줄 몰랐어요.

B 그는 이 회사에 영업사원으로 겨우 1년 있었어요. 그렇게 짧은 기간 내에 어떻게 그런 위치로 승진할 수가 있어요?

A 무슨 말인지 알겠어요. 하지만, 지금까지 훌륭하게 일하고 있잖아요. 그가 우리 회사에 입사한 이래로 매출이 상당량 증가했어요. 전 그가 그럴 자격이 된다고 봐요.

B 그건 당신 생각이죠. 이 일로 많은 직원들이 의기소침해질 거예요.

C 1 ⓓ 2 ⓐ

WEEK 12 | 직원 평가 및 직무와 책임

Vocabulary Check-up p.109

A 1 ⓑ 2 ⓐ 3 ⓔ 4 ⓒ 5 ⓓ

B 1 supposed 2 handle 3 have got 4 take on
  5 hard-working

C 1 take care 2 take the blame 3 think
  4 much credit 5 charge of

Conversation 1 직원 평가하기 p.110   57.mp3

A: 자, 6개월 동안 부장을 맡아왔는데, 여기서 근무하는 거 어땠어요?

B: 일은 괜찮고 전문적이에요. 그런데 부하 직원과 문제가 있으리라곤 생각하지 못했어요. 특히, 윌리엄요.

A: 그 사람 똑똑하지 않아요?

B: 그가 똑똑하지 않다는 게 아니라 조직과 조화를 못 이룬다는 거예요. 항상 자신만의 방식으로 일하려고 해요.

A: 케니는 어때요?

B: 윌리엄만큼 똑똑하지 않아요. 하지만 매우 체계적이고 팀의 구성원으로 함께 일하는 법을 알고 있어요. 저는 윌리엄을 팀 안에서 일할 필요가 없는 다른 업무로 이전시키려고 생각 중이에요.

Conversation 2 직무와 책임 p.111   58.mp3

A: 존 로우라는 고객으로부터 불만을 접수했어요. 그가 받지도 않은 선적물에 우리가 대금청구서를 보냈다고 하더군요. 뭐가 잘못된 거죠, 프레드?

B: 어디서 발생된 문제인지 모르겠는데요. 확인하고 연락 드릴게요. … 낸시, 다이애나가 실수했더군요.

A: 알다시피 올해 들어 세 번째예요. 당신이 선적부서 관리자니까 책임을 지세요. 직원들의 일과를 체크하는 것이 당신 업무잖아요.

B: 네, 제 책임입니다. 직원들을 교육시켜서 그들의 업무가 얼마나 중요한지 깨닫게 하겠습니다.

Practice 1 Let's Speak p.112

A 1 You should take the blame for your actions.
  2 I didn't expect to become so close to my team members.
  3 You should accept responsibility as a human resource manager.
  4 He is responsible for checking the inventory status on a daily basis.
  5 My boss always wants to do things thoroughly.
  6 She is not as organized or meticulous as Sally.

B 1 ⓑ 2 ⓐ 3 ⓔ 4 ⓓ 5 ⓒ

Practice 2 Listen-up p.113

Audio Script – A, B   59.mp3

Kevin	I'm at my wit's end, Alicia.
Alicia	You have a great job. You are making decent money. Kevin, what's the problem?
Kevin	Here's my problem. I can't stand my boss, and I'm quite sure he feels the same way about me. We don't communicate well, and he is always criticizing me.
Alicia	Yeah, I know he is very demanding and dismissive.
Kevin	You can say that again. In addition, he is a terrible listener.
Alicia	I heard that our executives are thinking of firing him. So don't worry, Kevin.

케빈 완전히 지쳐버렸어요, 앨리시아.

앨리시아 좋은 직업을 가졌지, 돈도 많이 벌지. 케빈, 뭐가 문제예요?

케빈 내 문제는 이거예요. 상사를 못 견뎌내겠어요. 그리고 그 사람도 나와 같은 심정일 거예요. 우린 의사소통이 잘 안 돼요, 그리고 그 사람은 언제나 나만 비난하죠.

앨리시아 그래요, 그 사람이 아주 요구가 많고 무시하는 성향이 있다는 거 알아요.

케빈 맞아요. 게다가, 엄청나게 남의 말을 안 들어요.

앨리시아 우리 임원진이 그 사람을 해고할 생각이라고 들었어요. 그러니까 걱정 말아요, 케빈.

A 1 False 2 True 3 False 4 True

B 1 making decent money 2 can't stand my boss
  3 don't communicate well 4 demanding and dismissive
  5 a terrible listener

Jordan	Have you finished the sales report, Kelly?
Kelly	No, not yet.
Jordan	Again? You know, it's always your job to prepare the report for the weekly meeting. Don't you think you're neglecting your work?
Kelly	Oh, it's not due till Friday, isn't it?
Jordan	It's due tomorrow, Kelly. Didn't you check your email yesterday? I informed you that the meeting was advanced to Thursday.
Kelly	Really? Oh, no. I thought your mail was spam and deleted it!
Jordan	How many times have I told you to look at the sender's name?
Kelly	I'm so sorry, Jordan. I should take the blame for it.
Jordan	Finish it by tomorrow no matter what happens.
Kelly	It won't happen again.

조단	영업 보고서 완성했어요, 켈리?
켈리	아니요, 아직요.
조단	또요? 주간 회의에 필요한 보고서를 준비하는 게 항상 당신 일이라는 거 알잖아요. 직무를 게을리한다는 생각 안 들어요?
켈리	어, 금요일까지잖아요, 그렇지 않아요?
조단	내일까지예요, 켈리. 어제 이메일 확인 안 했어요? 회의가 목요일로 앞당겨졌다고 알렸잖아요.
켈리	정말요? 이런. 스팸 메일인 줄 알고 지웠는데!
조단	보낸 사람 이름을 확인하라고 몇 번이나 얘기했어요?
켈리	죄송해요, 조단. 제 잘못이에요.
조단	무슨 일이 있어도 내일까지 끝내요.
켈리	다신 이런 일 없도록 할게요.

C   **1** neglecting   **2** sales report   **3** email

PLUS WEEK \ 반박과 호응 및 다양한 삽입어

Vocabulary Check-up p.115

A **1** ⓑ **2** ⓐ **3** ⓓ **4** ⓔ **5** ⓒ

B **1** has nothing **2** make sense **3** can relate
    4 differently **5** In addition

C **1** By the way **2** other hand **3** particularly[especially]
    4 like **5** As far

Conversation 1 반박하기 p.116   61.mp3

A: 배터리가 없는 노트북을 만들 계획이에요.
B: 터무니없군요. 당신들이 하는 일에는 상관 안 합니다. 항상 이상한 생각만 들고 나오잖아요.
A: 이번엔 대박일 거라고 정말 확신하는데요!
B: 소비자 여론조사 했다고 그랬죠? 소비자들은 명백히 배터리를 원한다고요. 그래야 전원 코드 없이 노트북을 쓸 수 있으니까요.
A: 흠, 그들은 또 싼 노트북을 원하죠.
B: 이봐요! 그래서 소비자들이 가격을 낮추고자 본질적인 기능을 제거하길 원한다고 생각해요?
A: 왜 우리 상품기획팀과 관련된 것이라면 뭐든지 부정적이죠?
B: 당신 팀에 부정적인 것이 아니라 그 생각들에 부정적인 거예요.

Conversation 2 다양한 삽입어 p.117   62.mp3

A: 제프, 우리 회사가 10억짜리 계약에 입찰 중이라고 들었어요.
B: 네. 우리가 가격 경쟁력이 있어서 유리하다고 생각해요.
A: 저도 그렇게 봅니다. 그건 그렇고, 고객들과 얼마나 자주 외식하시죠?
B: 한 달에 평균 두 번이요. 왜요?
A: 우리 임원들은 우리가 고객 접대에 돈을 너무 많이 쓴다고 생각해요.
B: 하지만 분명히 그럴 만한 가치가 있습니다. 실제로, 일주일 전에 닷컴 회사와 수십 억짜리 계약을 맺었잖아요.
A: 그렇다면 정말 값어치가 있네요.
B: 게다가, 또 다른 광고 건을 논의하러 그 사람들이 다음 주에 방문할 거예요.

Practice 1 Let's Speak p.118

A **1** expand / differently **2** build / sure **3** break / say
    4 attractive / point

B **1** In fact, he is negative about the company's sales plan.
    2 Even though it's new, this calculator doesn't function properly.
    3 Besides, this service saves a lot of time and money.
    4 We will hold the seminar unless it rains.
    5 By the way, why are we losing our market share?
    6 As long as you're on our team, you should follow the policy of our team.

Logan	Can I have a word with you, Katharina?
Katharina	Sure. What's up, Logan?
Logan	We must decide the date of the launch as soon as possible. When are we going to launch the Smartphone?
Katharina	Personally, I'm in favor of September.
Logan	Shouldn't we wait till the winter?
Katharina	Why wait any longer?
Logan	It's a peak period for buying mobile phones.
Katharina	It doesn't make sense to me. Why should we have to wait another three months? Let's just cash in on that as early as possible.

로건	얘기 좀 할까요, 카타리나?
카타리나	네. 무슨 일이죠, 로건?
로건	가능한 한 빨리 출시일을 잡아야 해서요. 스마트폰을 언제 출시할까요?
카타리나	개인적으로 9월이 좋겠는데요.
로건	겨울까지 기다려야 하지 않을까요?
카타리나	왜 더 기다려야 하죠?
로건	겨울이 휴대전화 구매의 성수기거든요.
카타리나	말도 안 돼요. 왜 3개월이나 더 기다려야 하나요? 그냥 가능한 한 빨리 돈을 법시다.

A 1 ⓒ 2 Winter.

B 1 have a word with you
    2 as soon as possible
    3 in favor of
    4 Shouldn't we wait
    5 doesn't make sense to me
    6 as early as possible

Lisa	Alan, what do you think the keys to success in online selling are?
Alan	First of all, we must understand why customers use online selling. Do you know why, Lisa?
Lisa	Well, they use online selling for lots of different reasons. Some people are using it to actually buy something. And other people are coming to a website to acquire information about a product.
Alan	That's for sure, Lisa. So the keys for us are making them visit our website more often by providing good information.
Lisa	Oh, before I forget, let's talk about the time for setting up the website. Where do we stand?
Alan	We're still working on it. When do you want to have it up and running?
Lisa	I want it in a month's time, which is the end of June.
Alan	That's a bit early.

리사	앨런, 인터넷 판매에서 성공하는 비결이 뭐라고 생각해요?
앨런	우선, 고객들이 왜 인터넷 판매를 이용하는지 이해해야죠. 왜 그런 줄 알아요, 리사?
리사	음, 고객들은 여러 가지 이유로 인터넷 판매를 이용하죠. 어떤 사람들은 실제로 물건을 구매하려고 이용하고, 어떤 사람들은 제품 정보를 얻으려고 웹사이트를 방문하죠.
앨런	맞아요, 리사. 그래서 우리의 성공 비결은 좋은 정보를 제공해서 사람들이 우리 웹사이트를 더 자주 방문하게 만드는 거예요.
리사	아차, 잊어버리기 전에, 웹사이트 제작 기간에 대해서 얘기 좀 하죠. 상황이 지금 어때요?
앨런	계속 작업 중이에요. 언제 운영을 시작할까요?
리사	저는 한 달 안에, 그러니까 6월 말까지는 끝났으면 하는데요.
앨런	좀 이르네요.

C 1 False 2 True 3 True 4 False

SPECIAL PART — 비즈니스 이메일
Business E-mail

UNIT 01 \ 의견 묻고 나누기

Vocabulary Check-up p.125

1 As we all know 2 too difficult for us
3 would help us know 4 grateful if you could
5 planning to develop

Writing Exercise p.128

A 1 We are planning to develop a coffee-flavored ice cream.
2 It is difficult for me to finish the report alone without any help within two days.
3 It would help us know why our customers complain about our service.
4 It would be grateful if you could let me have your comments and advice on that matter.
5 It is difficult to comment on this type of situation because everyone has different views about that.
6 I don't think it is important to find out who is responsible for the sales reduction.
7 I don't have an opinion on who will be the next CEO of our company.
8 In my personal opinion, we are not ready to take on a huge project yet.

B 1 we are planning to develop /
Please let me know your opinion
2 Our website is now under construction /
Please share your ideas
3 It is difficult to comment on the website /
Could you provide us with some detailed information

UNIT 02 \ 동의하기 또는 반대하기

Vocabulary Check-up p.131

1 agree with you 2 with your suggestion
3 move / back to 4 asked / call me
5 do my part

Writing Exercise p.134

A 1 Due to the bad weather conditions here, we moved the meeting back till the end of July.
2 He ordered me to go in early and prepare everything for the meeting.
3 I wholeheartedly agree with you that we should fire the workers.
4 I will do my part by encouraging our workers to work hard until the project is complete.
5 I am in total agreement with your decision to reject their request.
6 I tend to agree with you, but what matters most is finding a way to escape from this depressing situation.
7 I don't mean to disagree with you, but I think we first have to know what is happening with our intranet system.
8 I'd like to propose that we consider offering free MP3 downloads of these recordings.

B 1 Thank you for hosting the workshop /
I agree with you that we will have to form a task force /
the names and job titles of the three persons
2 Thank you for your opinion /
I don't mean to disagree with you, but
3 I don't think it is easy to add a recording function /
I would like to propose that we add it

Vocabulary Check-up p.137

1 eagerly waiting for   2 will be done
3 never heard the news   4 Please keep in mind
5 careful not to

Writing Exercise p.140

A 1 Our stock fell after the deal was done.
2 I heard the news that you are leaving the company because of your health condition.
3 We are eagerly waiting for the new model of the lower price.
4 Please keep in mind that there have been some concerns about your working style.
5 Let this serve as a fair warning: We will not put up with your violating our rules.
6 We are very disappointed to learn that you do not intend to participate in the workshop.
7 Please accept our sincerest apology for the technical glitches that happened on your website.
8 The difficulty lies in finding the right solution to this problem.

B 1 We are very disappointed to learn that /
We cannot make any firm decision
2 Let this serve as a fair warning /
This is your last chance to /
legal action against our company
3 we are sorry for the miscommunication /
The difficulty lies in the fact that we are working

Vocabulary Check-up p.143

1 hate / trouble you   2 should prepare for
3 I was informed   4 not good at
5 greatly helpful / advise

Writing Exercise p.146

A 1 We are preparing for the upcoming workshop held at Michigan State University.
2 I don't want to bother you, but I would like to ask for your help.
3 I would really appreciate it if you could instruct me how to send an email.
4 I was informed that you are knowledgeable about the travel industry.
5 It would be greatly helpful if you could tell me whom I should ask regarding this matter.
6 I would like you to tell me how to better use this program.
7 I would like to ask your advice on how to book tickets in advance.
8 I advise you to work with him to finish the report on time.

B 1 It would be greatly helpful if you could specifically advise me
2 We were very impressed with /
we decided to take your advice and closed the bank account
3 I would like you to listen to me more /
you should take it seriously

English for Business Communication 시리즈

General Business Practical Business International Business

English for Business Communication 시리즈는 전 3권에 걸쳐 비즈니스 업무 진행에 필수적인 영어 표현들을 습득할 수 있도록 구성하였습니다.

General Business 비즈니스 일상 영어

출퇴근 인사를 비롯하여 동료 간의 커뮤니케이션을 위한 일상 표현들과, 비즈니스 업무의 기본인 전화 응대, 약속 잡기, 외국손님 맞이, 해외 출장 등에 관련한 영어 표현들을 익힙니다.

Practical Business 사내 실무 영어

좀 더 실질적인 업무 처리를 요하는 프레젠테이션 상황, 회의, 업무 지시 및 보고, 의견 제안 및 설득 등 효과적인 커뮤니케이션을 위한 핵심적인 영어 표현들을 다룹니다.

International Business 비즈니스 국제 영어

회사 간 무역 거래, 계약 및 협상, 마케팅 협의, 예산과 재정 관리 등 대외적인 업무 처리에 필요한 영어 표현들을 익힙니다.

Overview

PART 1 비즈니스 전화 Business Telephoning

Week	Title	Overview
WEEK 01	전화 걸고 받기 Making and Answering a Call	• 전화 관련 기본 어휘 익히기 to know basic vocabulary for telephone • 전화 걸고 받기 to make & answer a call • 전화 바꿔주기 to transfer a call
WEEK 02	메시지 남기고 받기 Leaving and Taking Messages	• 전화를 받을 수 없는 이유 말하기 to say why he or she is not in • 언제 통화가 가능한지 묻기 to ask when he or she is available • 메시지 남기고 받기 to leave or take a message
WEEK 03	잘못 걸린 전화와 자동응답기 Wrong Calls and Answering Machine	• 통화를 하려는 사람 찾기 to look for someone • 잘못 걸린 전화에 대응하기 to respond to the wrong number • 자동응답기에 용건 남기기 to leave a message to the answering machine
PLUS WEEK	통화 중 문제 발생과 국제전화 Problems with the Phone and International Calls	• 전화기 문제에 대처하기 when having problems with the phone • 전화 통화 다음으로 미루기 to get back to someone later • 국제전화 걸기 to make international calls

PART 2 사무실에서의 일상 업무 Daily Routines at the Office

Week	Title	Overview
WEEK 04	미팅 약속 정하기 Making an Arrangement for Meeting	• 약속 정하기 to set up an appointment • 약속 변경하기 to reschedule an appointment • 약속 취소하기 to cancel an appointment
WEEK 05	출퇴근 인사와 휴가 신청 Greeting at Work and Asking for Leave	• 아침 출근인사 하기 to greet in the morning when you get to work • 조퇴 사유 말하기 to say why you leave work • 휴가 신청하기 to asking for a day off
WEEK 06	감사와 격려 표현하기 Expressing Appreciation and Encouragement	• 감사와 축하 표하기 to show appreciation and to congratulate someone • 격려하기 to encourage someone • 위로하기 to express one's condolences to someone
PLUS WEEK	사무기기 다루기 Dealing with Office Equipment	• 사무용품 빌리기 to borrow office supplies • 컴퓨터 문제 해결하기 to troubleshoot a computer problem • 복사기 문제 해결하기 to troubleshoot a photocopier problem

SPECIAL PART 비즈니스 이메일 Business E-mail

Unit	Title	Overview
UNIT 01	첫 비즈니스 이메일 보내기 Sending a Business E-mail for the First Time	• 이메일의 목적 말하기 to tell the purpose of e-mail • 자기 소개하기 to introduce myself • 맺음말 알기 to know the concluding remarks
UNIT 02	첨부파일 보내기 Enclosing an Attachment	• 첨부파일 보내기 to enclose an attachment • 파일 여는 방법 알려주기 to tell how to view the file • 유의사항 전달하기 to give previous notice

Overview

PART 1 국제 무역 International Trade

Week	Title	Overview
WEEK 01	제품 정보 얻기 Obtaining Information about Products	• 제품 사양에 대해 묻기 Asking about a product's specifications • 제품 특징에 대해 말하기 Talking about a product's features • 자료 요청하기 Requesting product information
WEEK 02	가격 인하 요청하기 Requesting a Price Reduction	• 가격에 대해 묻기 Asking about prices • 가격 비교하기 Comparing prices • 할인 요청하기 Asking for a discount
WEEK 03	주문과 배송 Order and Delivery	• 주문하기 Placing an order • 제품 배송하기 Delivering products • 품질보증에 대해 묻기 Asking about warranties
PLUS WEEK	클레임 처리하기 Dealing with Claims	• 불만 표시하기 Making complaints • 고객 불만에 대처하기 Handling complaints • 불만사항 해결하기 Solving complaints

PART 2 협상 Negotiation

Week	Title	Overview
WEEK 04	교섭자 맞이하기 Greeting Negotiators	• 소개하기 Making introductions • 가벼운 이야기 나누기 Making small talk • 협상 절차 설명하기 Explaining the negotiation procedure
WEEK 05	입장 밝히기 Establishing Positions	• 협상 안건 확인하기 Confirming the negotiation agenda • 입장을 명확하게 취하기 Clarifying your position • 입장 정리하기 Summarizing each position
WEEK 06	제안하기와 흥정하기 Making Proposals and Bargaining	• 제안하기 Making proposals • 대안 제시하기 Making counterproposals • 흥정하기 Bargaining
PLUS WEEK	갈등 대처하기와 협상 끝내기 Handling Conflicts and Closing a Negotiation	• 강력하게 주장하기 Insisting on your opinion • 해결책 찾기 Creating solutions • 계약 체결하기 Closing a contract

SPECIAL PART 비즈니스 이메일 Business E-mail

Unit	Title	Overview
UNIT 01	제품에 관한 문의 Questions about Products	• 제품 사양 설명하기 Explaining a product's specifications • 카탈로그 및 견본 보내기 Sending catalogs and sample products
UNIT 02	주문하기 Placing an Order	• 주문하기 Placing an order • 주문을 취소하거나 변경하기 Canceling or changing an order • 선적 및 대금 정보 받기 Obtaining shipping/payment information